The USA
A Divided Union

NEIL DEMARCO

GENERAL EDITOR: JOSH BROOMAN

6

Addison Wesley Longman Limited
Edinburgh Gate, Harlow,
Essex CM20 2JE, England
and Associated Companies throughout the world.

First published 1994
Sixth impression 1998

ISBN 0 582 22674 0

Set in Concorde and Tecton

Produced by Addison Wesley Longman China Limited, Hong Kong.
GCC/06

The publisher's policy is to use paper manufactured from sustainable forests.

Design and Production by Hart Mcleod, Cambridge

Illustrations by Sheila Betts

Cover Instruments of power from *American Today, 1930, by* Thomas Hart Benton.
© Collection, The Equitable Life Assurance Society of the US.
Photograph: Bridgeman Art Libary.

Acknowledgements

We are grateful to the following for permission to reproduce photographs. The numbers
refer to page numbers.

The Advertising Archives, 15; Associated Press, 79; Bettmann Archive, 31; British Film
Institute, 29; Carpenter Center for the Visual Arts, Harvard University (Photo courtesy
Fotofolio, Inc.), 91; Culver Pictures, 25 top; from the *Daily Mail*, London, 24 October 1962,
courtesy the *Daily Mail*, 104; E.T. Archive, 11, 12 left, 68 right; Mary Evans Picture
Library, 16, 18 right; courtesy Larry Gonick, 34; © Est. Thomas Hart Benton/DACS
London/VAGA New York 1994, 7; Hulton-Deutsch Collection, 44, 66, 74 left; Imperial
War Museum, London, 12 centre & right; Kobal Collection, 84; from the original painting
The Golden Spike by Mort Künstler, copyright 1985 Mort Künstler, Inc., 5; Library of
Congress, 41, 71; Colin McArthur, 56, 62, 93; cartoon by Ross Lewis from the *Milwaukee
Journal*, 1948, 74 right; National Archives, Washington DC, 45 bottom, 55, 58 bottom;
Peter Newark's Pictures, 14, 43, 58 top, 63 left, 89; from the *News Chronicle*, 16 April 1952,
courtesy Associated Newspapers Group Ltd., 68 left; Northwestern University Library,
Special Collections Department, 32; cartoon by Jerry Doyle from the *Philadelphia Daily
News*, 3 March 1993, 38; Popperfoto, 9, 21, 22, 35, 36, 45 top, 63 right, 77, 80, 103; cartoon
by Norman Mansbridge from *Punch*, 20 September 1961, courtesy *Punch*, 102; Redferns,
86; Rex/Sipa/O.C.R. Rodriguez, 111 bottom; Smithsonian Institution (neg. no. 55,297), 6;
Topham Picture Source, 67, 95, 106; Frank Spooner/Gamma/R. Rotola, 111 top; UPI/
Bettmann, 19 bottom, 20, 27, 33, 60, 70, 97, 99; *Vogue* © The Condé Nast Publications Ltd.,
18 left, 19 top; Weidenfeld & Nicolson Archives, 49 left.

The written sources in this book are taken from many different kinds of published
material. Some were originally written in old-fashioned or unusual language. In most
cases, unusual or difficult words are explained in the margin. In the rare cases where this
has not been possible the wording has been slightly adapted. In many of the sources
words have been left out. A cut in the middle of a sentence is shown like this…; and at
the end of a sentence like this ….

We are grateful to International Music Publications Ltd for permission to reproduce the
lyrics of 'C'Mon Everybody'. Words and Music by Jerry N. Capehart and Eddie Cochran.
© 1959 Unart Music Corp., USA. Burlington Music Co Ltd, London.

Contents

THE UNITED STATES OF AMERICA

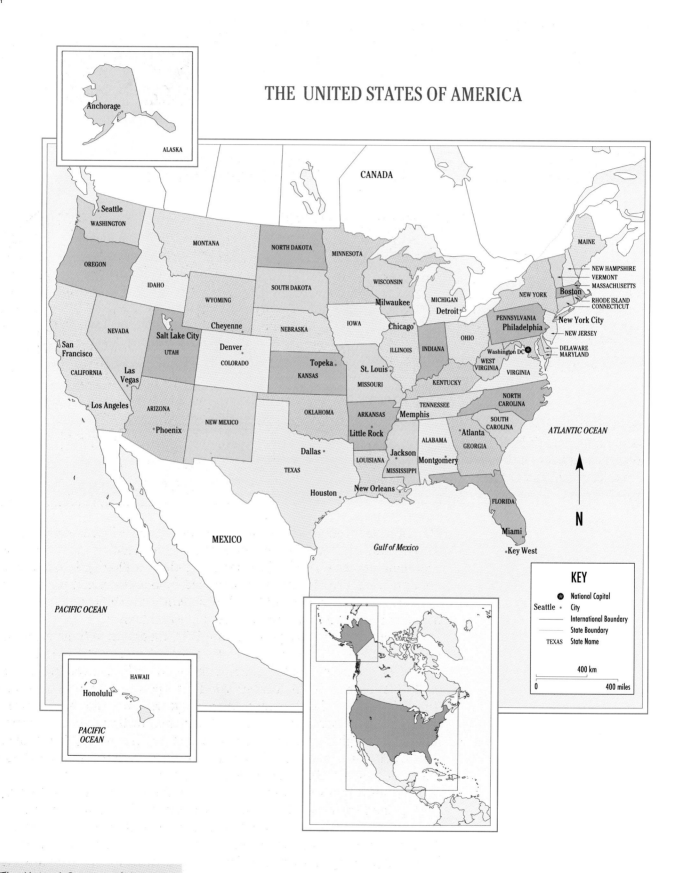

The United States of America

Introduction

The United States: from sleeping giant to superpower

Source 1

Railways meet! The Golden Spike ceremony at Promontory Point, Utah, in 1869. American businessmen gather around as the final spike is driven in to link the last rail into position. This completed the railway route across the vast continent of North America.

■ This scene was painted in 1985. What does it suggest about how Americans still saw their past?

The Twentieth century has seen tremendous changes in the world we live in. The United States began this century as a 'sleeping giant'. Its huge economic power was only just becoming clear. Militarily, it still seemed unimpressive. The US fleet was described by one American politician at the time as a collection of 'old washtubs'. World power lay in the hands of the great European states: Britain, Germany and France.

Gradually, the military power of the USA caught up with its economic might. Its role was decisive in two world wars (1914–1918 and 1939–1945), and the United States then found itself involved in a deadly confrontation with the only other world superpower, the Soviet Union (or 'Russia', unofficially). For more than 45 years the 'Cold War' between these two countries and their allies threatened to bring about a terrible nuclear war which would destroy the planet. By the end of 1991, though, the Soviet Union had ceased to exist as a single country, and the United States was the world's unchallenged great power.

The painting above (Source 1) shows the ceremony in which the final, golden spike was driven in to complete the first railway linking the east and west coasts of America. The picture celebrates many things in American history. It celebrates the growing unity of the USA achieved by its ever-expanding network of railways. It celebrates the tremendous drive and inventiveness of the railway engineers who triumphed over huge engineering problems, building tracks over the vast prairies and through the Rocky Mountains. It also celebrates America's triumph over the last untamed 'frontier' – Americans now felt that they had brought 'civilisation' to the whole continent.

The painting is also a rather romantic view of America's past and one which not all Americans share. To American Indians it represents the theft of their land and the destruction of their way of life, as the railway brought settlers and towns deep into their homelands. It shows that there are two ways of looking at 'progress'. For some people, change is not always something to be welcomed. The years between 1917 and 1963 continued to see great changes, and with these changes came further conflict and division.

This book investigates how the USA was transformed into the most influential and powerful country in the world. It investigates how the world's richest nation also became a very divided one. The causes of this division between rich and poor, and between white and black, will form an important theme of this book.

Source 2

Arapaho Indians doing a Ghost Dance in their reservation, 1893. They were recalling a traditional way of life which had been virtually destroyed by white Americans in the Nineteenth century. Change and progress for some people brought conflict and suffering to others. Divisions within the United States remain deep-seated up to the present day.

Unit 1 · A decade of extremes

Source 1

This mural by Thomas Hart Benton is titled *Entertainment*. The period after the First World War was one of new freedom and excitement for many – hence the phrase The Roaring Twenties.

When the First World War broke out in Europe in 1914, the USA was determined to keep out, and it did so – until April 1917. After the war, Americans once again turned their backs on political events in Europe. They were more interested in events in their own country, and particularly their economy. These were prosperous years for many Americans, and the economy flourished as never before. In the early and middle 1920s businesses expanded, jobs were created, and living standards rose. The problems of poverty and the slums seemed less important in these years of boom.

Women made important progress in creating a more equal role for themselves during and after the war. Ideas about how women should behave began to change, too. Attitudes to black people, though, did not change noticeably – despite the active role black troops had played in the war. In fact, the racist organisation, the Ku Klux Klan (see pages 22–24), reached its peak of 5 million members in 1923.

The ten years after the First World War were a decade of extremes – of wealth and poverty, of racist violence, of temperance (no alcohol) and gangland killings, and of changing manners. This unit looks at America's entry into the war, and at aspects of the remarkable decade that followed.

1.1 The USA enters the First World War

A policy of isolation

Traditionally, the USA followed a policy of 'isolation'. This meant that it preferred to keep out of international affairs. At the outbreak of the First World War, the USA was already the most powerful nation in the world – in terms of a vast population and industry. But it was not interested in becoming involved in European quarrels, nor in a war thousands of kilometres away, fighting for a remote cause.

From isolation to involvement

When the fighting broke out between the Allies (France, Belgium, Britain, Serbia and Russia) and the Central Powers (Germany and Austria-Hungary) in August 1914, the United States remained neutral. President Woodrow Wilson confirmed his opposition to the war during the presidential election in 1916. He won the election for the Democratic Party with 3 million votes more than his rival, using the slogan: 'He kept us out of war'. There was no doubting the hostility of the American people to any involvement with Europe's war. Yet in April 1917, just four months later, the United States declared war on Germany.

There were three major reasons for this change of attitude. Firstly, from February 1917, the Germans began sinking US merchant ships trading with Britain. The Germans had decided to take the risk of provoking American anger; they hoped to win a quick 'knock-out' victory in the war, 'starving' the British into surrender. All ships in the war zone – whether enemy or neutral – would be sunk by German submarines without warning.

Secondly, Wilson had good reason to suspect that the Germans were preparing for war with America anyway. In March, the news broke that a secret message from Germany to Mexico had been decoded. In the message, Germany promised that if war *did* break out between itself and the USA, Germany would help Mexico recover its 'lost territory' in the USA – the states of Texas, New Mexico and Arizona – if Mexico helped the Germans in return.

Finally, Wilson believed that if the Allies won the war with US support, America could play an important role in shaping a settlement at the end of the war. He had passionate ideals. He believed strongly that this would ensure future peace, and 'make the world safe for democracy'.

Americans at war: at the frontline

American troops played a crucial role in the fighting in Europe. They took part in the Allied offensives of 1918, which finally drove the Germans back and led to their surrender in November. There were 1.7 million US soldiers in Europe by the time the war ended. They were fresh and eager, giving the tired Allied troops a timely boost after four years of fighting. The knowledge that the whole US industrial strength was behind the Allies also helped to break German morale. In total, 120,000 American soldiers were killed or died of disease at the Front, and some 200,000 were wounded.

The role of the US Navy was also significant in the war effort. The Allies had lost 900,000 tonnes of shipping by April 1917. By April 1918, with the help of US convoys, the loss had dropped to just 200,000 tonnes. This meant that Germany's gamble of starving Britain into defeat by cutting off vital supplies had failed.

Black soldiers at war

There were 400,000 US troops in France by the time the war ended. Black soldiers were almost all used for labouring duties, away from the fighting, and were kept in all-black units. There were a few black officers, but none were ever allowed to command white troops.

Source 2

This US Army poster from the 1930s shows determined black soldiers advancing on the enemy, bayonets at the ready.

■ This poster suggested that black soldiers were used for combat roles. Did their experience of the First World War support this?

The Germans tried to persuade black troops to desert and change sides. They scattered leaflets over the trenches where the black soldiers were positioned, and tried to convince them that black people should not be fighting for a country which treated them so badly.

Source 3

Extract from a leaflet dropped by the Germans over the trenches in France where black American troops were positioned in 1918.

What is democracy? Personal freedom, all citizens enjoying the same rights socially and before the law. Do you enjoy the same rights as the white people do in America, the land of Freedom and Democracy, or are you treated over there as second-class citizens? Can you go into a restaurant where white people dine? Can you get a seat in the theatre where white people sit? Is lynching* a lawful activity in a democratic country?

lynching Killing by a mob – often by hanging – without a fair trial.

In many of the Southern States black people were kept apart from white people. They were not allowed to use the same restaurants or theatres as whites. Lynching did take place and usually went unpunished. Despite the truth of German propaganda (Source 3), no black troops deserted their lines to go over to the Germans. Their loyalty was to go unrewarded by an ungrateful America after the war.

America at war: the home front

In 1917, the whole nation had to be mobilised for war on a massive scale. The government was forced to play a new and active role to ensure that American industry increased its output of war supplies. It settled disputes between workers and employers to stop strikes in war industries; it increased taxes to pay for the war. There were huge propaganda campaigns to encourage the public to save food. The government organised 'Meatless Tuesdays' and 'Wheatless Mondays', as well as the planting of victory gardens. 'Food will win the war' was the slogan.

President Wilson also set up the Committee on Public Information (CPI) to organise propaganda. Its aim was to promote the view that America was defending democracy and civilisation against barbaric 'Huns' (an insulting term for Germans). The German sinking of a British passenger liner, the *Lusitania*, in May 1915 was used as an example of 'Hunnish barbarity'. Among the 1,200 passengers who drowned were 128 Americans.

The propaganda was very effective; people started associating 'German' with 'disloyalty'. In many areas of the USA, the teaching of German in schools, and the playing of music by German composers, was banned.

Wilson and the peace settlement

On 11 November 1918, the fighting finally stopped, and the Germans surrendered to the Allies. In January 1918, Wilson put forward Fourteen Points which he said should form the basis of a peace settlement to end the war. The British and the French objected to them, though, because they thought they were too generous to the Germans.

Eventually, in 1919, a series of treaties was signed in Paris with each of the defeated nations. The most important of these was the Treaty of Versailles with Germany. In the talks leading to the treaties, Wilson tried to ensure that the various nationalities of Europe had their own countries. The Poles, for example, were given their own country of Poland. Wilson tried to stop the French and the British insisting on very harsh terms against the Germans, so that a future war of revenge would be less likely.

The League of Nations

One of Wilson's Fourteen Points called for a League of Nations to be set up. This would settle disputes between countries peacefully. America would play a role in maintaining world peace in the future. This idea was accepted by Britain and France, but not by the US Congress (see also pages 47–48 on the American political system). It voted against US membership of the League, even though the President was in favour, so Wilson had to accept this.

The reasons why so many Americans opposed the League were varied. Although they had taken part in the war, many Americans remained isolationist at heart. This meant that they wanted to avoid any commitments or treaties which might drag the United States into another 'European' war. American soldiers, they argued, should only be used where American interests were involved. This was a view common among Republican opponents of Wilson.

Some Democrats were also against joining the League because they were unhappy with the way it seemed designed to prop up the old empires of Britain and France. Many Americans remembered that they had won their freedom by going to war with the British Empire in 1776.

How were Americans persuaded to support the war?

If so many Americans were isolationists, why did they go to war in 1917 and fight with such enthusiasm? One answer may be found by looking at the propaganda of the US Government. Propaganda is the method used by governments or organisations to persuade people to believe certain things, or behave in a certain way. Sometimes, but not always, propaganda deliberately misleads.

The following posters were all produced on behalf of the government to get the American people supporting the war against Germany. This was necessary because at the beginning of 1917 very few Americans wanted to go to war. How do these posters help us to understand how American attitudes to the war were changed?

The US Government had to persuade people to lend money to help pay for the war by buying 'liberty bonds'. After the war those who had lent money would be repaid with interest. The liberty bond poster (Source 4) shows a nearly demolished Statue of Liberty amid the blazing ruins of New York harbour. The bombers in the sky are German.

Source 4

Wartime government poster. The words 'That Liberty Shall Not Perish From The Earth' are taken from a speech by President Abraham Lincoln in 1863.

■ Why do you think the bonds were called 'liberty bonds'?

THAT LIBERTY SHALL NOT
PERISH FROM THE EARTH
BUY LIBERTY BONDS
F O U R T H   L I B E R T Y   L O A N

A recruiting poster (Source 5) shows Germany as a 'mad brute'. Wearing a German army helmet, the brute carries a club representing German culture in one hand, and the American figure of Liberty in the other.

The government wanted people to feel able to help the war effort in many different ways so that everyone could do their bit for the boys 'over there' (in France). Source 6 gives an example of one of the ways the government encouraged people to help.

Some American civilians had been killed at sea by German U-boat attacks. Source 7 shows a drowning mother and baby, possibly from the *Lusitania*, a passenger liner sunk in 1915.

Source 6

A poster asking Americans to donate books to the army for soldiers to read in camp or at the Front.

Source 5

An army recruiting poster.

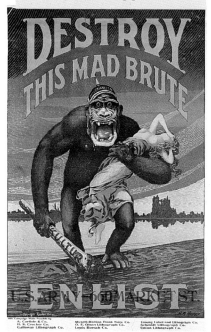

Source 7

A recruiting poster.

Questions

1 How would each of these posters (Sources 4–7) have encouraged Americans to support the US war effort?

2 Which one do you think would have had the most impact on the American public at that time? Why?

3 Which one of the posters do you think the Committee for Public Information would have liked most? Explain your answer.

4 Source 5 is obviously biased. Does this mean it is of no value to an historian?

1.2 The 1920s: more of everything

The US economy after the war

In 1913 the USA produced about 32 per cent of the world's industrial goods – more than Britain and Germany put together. It was a country rich in natural resources, such as coal, iron, oil, forests and fertile land. It needed to import very little and most of what it produced could be sold to its rapidly growing population.

Steel output is an important measure of a country's industrial strength. It is also a vital part of military strength. The output of the major world powers (Source 1) shows just how powerful the US economy was by 1920 – especially when compared to a Europe struggling to recover from the effects of the First World War.

Source 1

Steel production (in millions of tonnes)

	1913	1920
USA	32	42
Britain	8	9
Germany	18	8
France	5	3

A new consumer society

From a fairly strong position in 1920, the economy picked up sharply in 1922 and there was a great business boom until 1929. The output of industry rose by over one-third. By 1929, America produced about 46 per cent of the world's industrial goods. Old values of thrift and saving gave way to new attitudes: spending money became almost a virtue. New methods of payment – by instalment – made it possible for many more people to buy consumer goods that previously had been out of their reach. Much of the improvement in the economy was due to more efficient methods of production, management techniques and new industries.

Source 2

Gross National Product (or GNP) The total wealth produced by a country.

The business boom, 1922–1929

Year	Gross National Product* (in $ billion)	Income per head ($)
1922	74	672
1929	104	857

Why did the economy grow so fast?

The boom in business was led by three new industries: motor vehicles; electricity and electrical goods; and chemicals. The increase in car production was particularly dramatic.

Cars, cars, cars!

Before 1909 only the very wealthy could afford a car. It was unthinkable that a 'mere' farmer or shopgirl, for example, might own a car. But this is just what happened within the next 20 years. Between 1909 and 1928, a staggering 15 million Ford Model Ts were built. For the first time ever, cars came within the reach of ordinary people. This was only made possible because Henry Ford, a motor engineer, revolutionised car production.

Henry Ford was the son of a pioneer farming couple – an Irish father and a Dutch mother. From an early age he took more interest in machines and tools than farming, and was fascinated by steam engines. In 1896 he built his first motor car. He founded the Ford Motor Company in 1903, and in 1909 started producing the Model T. It was a runaway success.

In the past, each car was hand-built. The car chassis (body) stood in one place, labourers fetched the various parts, and skilled mechanics used them to build the car. But this method was slow. Henry Ford devised a new method to mass-produce cars. A conveyor belt and gravity slides moved all the materials and parts from one end of the factory to the other. Each worker had his own task to do, over and over again.

Henry Ford's new 'moving assembly line' meant that cars could be made in greater numbers, and therefore more cheaply than before. This boosted sales enormously. A Ford Model T cost $1,200 in 1909, but only $290 in 1925 (less than three months' wages for the average worker), and Ford was turning out 9,000 cars a day.

Source 3

Model Ts being mass-produced at a Ford factory, Highland Park, 1913. Gravity slides and chain conveyors helped in the mass-production of cars.

■ What evidence is there in the picture that the same workers did not build the car from start to finish, but did the same job all day?

The motor industry created a huge demand for steel, rubber, glass and oil, and all these industries boomed as a result. Roads had to be built for the cars to travel on, and this created yet more jobs. The cars needed petrol to run on, boosting the oil industry too.

Machines in the home

Domestic equipment such as refrigerators, vacuum cleaners and washing machines were also mass-produced in the 1920s. This led to a fall in prices, which encouraged people to spend more money and led to more employment.

The start of radio broadcasting in 1921 created a huge demand for radio sets. This in turn boosted the electrical industry. Radio sales rose from less than $2 million a year in 1920 to $600 million in 1929. The sale of radios fuelled the boom.

Real wages rose by 11 per cent by 1929. This meant that wages went up 11 per cent more than inflation. If people did not have the cash immediately, they could always buy items on credit through easy payment terms.

The atmosphere across the country was one of busy activity, and there was a sense that business would ensure that America stayed prosperous. Making money was almost a religious duty. 'The man who builds a factory builds a temple,' said Calvin Coolidge, President from 1923 to 1929.

A boom in advertising

At the turn of the century, advertising was restrained and politely informative. In the 1920s, advertising techniques became more sophisticated to persuade consumers to part with yet more money. The *National Advertiser* stated that 'One reason there's so much success in America is because there's so much advertising of things to want – things to work for.' However, some of the claims made by advertisers would be illegal today. The makers of Lucky Strike cigarettes, for example, claimed their product protected the voice and stopped coughing!

A grim contrast

The boom years did not benefit everyone. Farmers, who made up 25 per cent of the population, were not so fortunate during the 1920s. There was less demand for their produce from Europe, and prices fell. Modern farming machinery and fertilisers were expensive, too. Some 600,000 farmers lost their farms in 1924. By 1929, about 12 million families had an average annual income of $1,500. This was considered to be below the 'poverty line'. (People are said to be living below the poverty line if they earn less than is required to provide the basic needs of life – such as a home and food.)

There was also great poverty and hardship among the unskilled 'new' immigrants in the big cities (see page 20), and among black people in the North and South.

Source 4

An early advertisement for *Coca Cola*. Slogans became increasingly important in the 1920s as advertising became more advanced.

Questions

1 Why did the US economy not depend on other countries for its prosperity?

2 How did mass-production boost the US economy in the 1920s?

3 Why do you think the motor industry was such an important part of the prosperity of the 1920s?

1.3 Women in society: a new freedom?

Changing fashions, changing manners

Before the First World War, women were expected to lead restricted lives. Upper class women wore full-length dresses, and their tight under-garments included whalebone corsets, which hampered their movements.

Young ladies were meant to behave modestly. They were usually accompanied when they went out by an older female acting as a chaperon. (A chaperon was an older or married woman who accompanied or supervised a young unmarried woman on social occasions. It would have been considered scandalous for a man and unmarried woman to meet alone, for whatever reason.) It was also socially unacceptable for women to smoke in public before the war – it was *illegal* in New York.

After the war and during the 1920s much changed – at least for middle class and upper class women. Many taboos disappeared. Women started to smoke in public: sales of cigarettes doubled during the decade. It became acceptable for women to drive, and take part in strenuous sport. Women also socialised with men more easily. Chaperons were abandoned. The pre-war waltz gave way to a more daring dance: the Charleston.

By the mid 1920s, women's fashions had been transformed. Hemlines shot up. Some women stopped wearing restrictive corsets – something which would have been quite shocking before the war. There was a complete rebellion against strict 'Victorian' dress codes.

Sources 1 and 2 show the contrast between pre-war ladies' fashions and those of the post-war eras:

Source 1

Upper class ladies wear their evening dresses in a fashion illustration of 1905. The society woman would have changed her dress at least four times a day.

1 What items of clothing and accessories are these ladies shown wearing?

2 How might clothes like these restrict women's lives?

Source 2

Women with the latest 'look', from American fashion drawings of 1924.

■ How had hairstyles and clothes changed since 1907 (Source 1)?

The vote at last

In 1920, after decades of campaigning, women finally won the vote throughout the USA. Before 1920, women had been able to vote in only four US states.

The suffrage campaign had begun as long ago as 1869, when Susan Brownell Anthony set up the American Woman Suffrage Association. The more militant tactics of women like Alice Paul, Anne Howard Shaw and Carrie Chapman Gatt made women's suffrage an important political issue in the 1910s.

Opponents of women's suffrage tried hard to convince public opinion that women were too stupid to use the vote sensibly. One pre-war leaflet showed a woman 'selling' her vote to an election candidate for a box of chocolates!

Source 3

Women suffragists picketing outside the White House, 1917. The suffrage campaign gained further momentum in the years just before and during the war.

■ President Wilson's aim was to 'make the world safe for democracy'. How does the women's placard show up the irony of Wilson's aim?

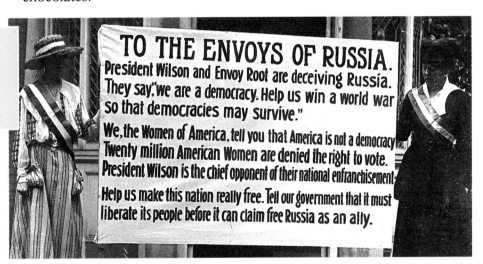

Women in the workplace

Traditionally, women were employed in 'female' areas of work such as domestic service, dress-making, clerical and secretarial work, nursing and teaching. (Of course, women also worked long hours in *unpaid* jobs – on the land and in the home.)

During the First World War, many women joined the workforce in new areas of work, to replace the men who were sent overseas to fight. Skilled factory work was new and welcome to many, but it did not last for long. Women workers were quickly replaced by the war veterans when they returned at the end of the fighting in 1918. Women who carried on working after the war found themselves forced back into 'women's' jobs, as before. They did not continue to enjoy the variety or choice of work they had experienced in wartime.

Despite this, there was a steady increase in the number of working women during the 1920s. The number of women in work increased 25 per cent during the decade, to 10.6 million in 1929. Women, though only middle class and upper class women, now had more opportunity to follow careers, rather than just work while waiting for a suitable husband. Their greater earning power in the 1920s attracted advertisers, eager to get women to spend on the new consumer goods available.

Was there a revolution in behaviour in the 1920s?

The following sources look at the fashions in clothes and behaviour for women in the 1920s. How far do they show a complete change from the pre-war era?

Vogue was a magazine which appealed to wealthy upper class women. Advertisers were keen to promote their products in it. Before the war, stockings had been made of very expensive silk. In the early 1920s, rayon – or artificial silk – put stockings within the reach of more women.

This illustration from the magazine *Judge* shows two young women out for a ride in the country with a young man.

Source 4

Advertisement for rayon stockings which appeared in *Vogue*, 1928.

■ What aspects of dress and behaviour in Sources 4 and 5 do you think would have been unacceptable before the war?

Source 5

Cover illustration from the magazine *Judge* in 1922.

The new fashions and behaviour of the 1920s were not restricted to large cities. The next source shows the concerns of a small rural college in the State of Idaho.

Source 6

Dress regulations at Northwest Nazarene College in Nampa, Idaho, early 1920s.

Thin dress materials may be used provided suitable underslips are worn. Skirts must be of such length as not to expose the calf of the leg. Flesh-colored or extremely thin hose are not permitted.

F. Scott Fitzgerald (1896–1940) is a well-known American writer. *This Side of Paradise* was his first novel and it was an instant success. In the novel, Fitzgerald describes the new post-war manners:

Source 7

From F. Scott Fitzgerald, *This Side of Paradise*, 1920. In this extract, the character Amory describes the scene.

None of the … mothers had any idea how casually their daughters were accustomed to be kissed. Amory saw girls doing things that even in his memory would have been impossible; eating at three-o'clock, after-dance suppers in impossible cafés, talking of every side of life ….

Changing attitudes after the war made it more socially acceptable for women to drive. Not many women could afford cars such as the one shown in Source 8, but companies clearly thought it was worth advertising such products for women.

Source 8

Advertisement for a Lincoln car, in *Vogue*, 1928

■ What image do the advertisers create for the car? How do they do this?

Every Lincoln body is a custom creation of some master body builder. It is designed as a fit companion piece for the Lincoln chassis. Its distinctive lines unmistakably suggest Lincoln quality. The Four Passenger Coupe is the work of Le Baron. The matchless performance of the Lincoln, its ease of control, its velvety smooth motor, its instantly responsive brakes and superb riding qualities are best of all appreciated in the owner-driven personal car.

L I N C O L N   M O T O R   C O M P A N Y
Division of Ford Motor Company

Questions

1. Explain how each of these sources (4–8) shows changes in social attitudes towards women, and attitudes held by women, in the 1920s.

2. What are the limitations of each of these sources (4–8)? Do they give a fair picture of changing attitudes?

3. Using Sources 1–8, comment on the view that 'The 1920s saw great changes in the social position of women.'

1.4 Racism in the 1920s

The 'new' immigrants

Source 1

Mass immigration: a ship packed with 'new' immigrants.

The American population grew rapidly during the 1920s – from 106 to 123 million. The major reason for this rapid increase was mass immigration. America had a long tradition of welcoming immigrants, and was proud of its rich 'melting pot' of peoples. For three centuries, immigrants had flooded into the USA: some came in flight from persecution, poverty and famine; others were attracted by the promise of a better life.

In the past, many immigrants had arrived from northern and western Europe, from countries of Anglo-Saxon stock like Britain, Ireland or Germany. Between 1900 and 1914, 13 million 'new' immigrants arrived in the United States, mostly from southern and eastern Europe. They included Italians, Hungarians, Poles, Czechs, Serbs and Greeks. Large ethnic communities grew up in the big cities – 'Little Italys' and 'Chinatowns' – while preserving their home traditions.

Resentment against these 'new' immigrants quickly built up. They were often poor. Many were illiterate and many could not speak English. Their cultural and religious background was different from that of the 'old' immigrants of northern and western Europe. They spoke very different languages, and they were often of different religions – Catholic or Jewish, rather than Protestant.

Immigrants and the 'Red Scare'
The working and living conditions of the 'new' immigrants were often very poor. Many suffered considerable hardship in their new home.

As they fought for better conditions, immigrants soon became associated with 'un-American' ideas, such as socialism and trade unionism. There were some bitter strikes in the mining, textile and steel industries just before the war, and troops were often used to break them. Strikes were thought to undermine the traditional American values of free enterprise and democracy.

After the war, a 'Red Scare' gripped the United States: immigrants, especially those from southern and eastern Europe, were often seen as criminals and Communist agents, stirring up industrial troubles. The treatment given to two Italian 'anarchists', Sacco and Vanzetti, was typical of the 'Red Scare' hysteria at the time. They were convicted, on slender evidence, of murder during a robbery in 1920. In 1927 they were executed by electric chair. Their real crime was that they had left-wing views and were foreigners.

Source 2

This cartoon of 1920 reflects the fear many people had of 'Reds' in America.

1 Who is the main character meant to represent?

2 Who is he holding?

WHOSE COUNTRY IS THIS, ANYHOW?

A clamp-down on immigration

The old, long-established immigrants from northern and western Europe soon succeeded in virtually banning immigration by these 'new' immigrants. In 1917, immigrants were forced to pass a literacy test to enter the USA. In the 1920s, three immigration acts were passed to limit the number of new immigrants per year, and to admit a greater proportion of people from Britain, Germany and Scandinavia, rather than from southern and eastern Europe. Ironically, the new laws left the door open to immigrants from Central and South America. Mexicans, Puerto Ricans and Cubans were now to become the fastest-growing ethnic minority.

This clamp-down on immigration was a drastic change of policy. The 'new' immigrants were no longer seen as enriching American culture. Apparently they had nothing good to offer. Behind the hostility to the newcomers lay religious prejudice and an assumption that Nordic peoples of the 'old' immigration were superior to the Slavic and Latin peoples of the new immigration.

Black people and the 'Jim Crow' laws

America's 12 million black people faced the Twentieth century with even more cause for despair. About 75 per cent of them lived in the South where they were discriminated against in housing, jobs and schooling. Few black people had the vote. 'Jim Crow' was an insulting term for a black person, and the Jim Crow laws forced them to use separate and inferior hotels, restaurants, buses and even water fountains. Lynch law ruled the South in the years after the First World War. In 1919 alone, 70 black people were lynched.

Source 3

Lynch law: the exact date of the photograph is unknown. These two black men were lynched in Indiana after they had been dragged from a local jail by a mob of 5,000 white townspeople. They had been arrested for the murder of a white man, but not yet tried. The impatient crowd decided the issue by hanging them.

■ What do the expressions on the faces in the crowd suggest or show?

Those black people who had hoped that war service would lead to greater opportunities and rights were quickly disappointed. About 1.5 million (out of 12 million) black people left the South, where there was little work and much discrimination, and headed for the North. They found themselves grouped in ghettos like New York's Harlem, but at least they had better prospects for work.

The Ku Klux Klan

The Ku Klux Klan, or KKK, was a terrorist and racist organisation in the USA. Its membership reached an all-time peak of about 5 million after the war, in 1923. The KKK's appeal spread beyond the traditionally 'racist' South to areas right across America, as far apart as Oregon and Maine. The Klan set out to keep blacks, Catholics, Jews and Mexicans 'in their place'. Only White, Anglo-Saxon Protestants (WASPs) could join the Klan. Those blacks – and whites – who tried to defend the rights of black people to equal treatment became victims of the Ku Klux Klan.

In fact, the KKK was more like a series of organisations, which changed in style over more than a century. In the 1920s, the KKK re-emerged in an even stronger and more widely-based form.

What was the appeal of the KKK?

The Klan's favourite methods of dealing with those black men and women it considered 'troublesome' included harassing, whipping, branding and lynching. Thousands of black people were hung by hooded white Klansmen without trial, while others were castrated. The flaming cross became the symbol of their terrorist activities, which the police and courts usually ignored. Why was such a hateful organisation so popular?

Source 4

KKK members are shown in Georgia waiting the arrival of their leader, the 'Imperial Wizard'.

■ What did the KKK 'uniform' consist of?

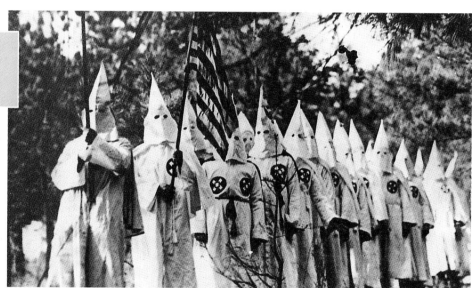

Part of their appeal in the 1920s was their secrecy, elaborate ceremonies and coded language (Sources 4 and 5). KKK officials had strange names such as 'Exalted Cyclops', 'Hydras' and 'King Kleagles'. From 1922, their leader was the 'Imperial Wizard', Hiram Evans. Klansmen sometimes spoke to each other in code. Here are a few examples:

Source 5

KKK secret language, from 'Konklave in Kokomo', by R. Coughlan.

■ Why did the KKK *need* or *want* a secret code?

Ayak – Are You A Klansman?

Akia – A Klansman I Am.

Sanbog – Strangers Are Near, Be On Guard.

What did the Klan stand for? KKK leaders like William Simmons made inflammatory speeches which found an eager audience:

Source 6

William J. Simmons, founder of the re-formed KKK, speaking in 1915.

[America] is a garbage can! ... When the hordes of aliens walk to the ballot box and their votes outnumber yours, then that alien horde has got you by the throat.

The largest groups of KKK members were in the South, the Southwest, the Midwest, California and Oregon. They mainly opposed blacks and Catholics, but also drunkards, gamblers, bootleggers (people who sold alcohol illegally), and people who they thought lowered moral standards.

For many Klansmen, like this one from Texas, the Klan was a vehicle for a wider moral crusade:

Source 7

Texan member of the Klan, speaking in the 1920s.

It [the KKK] is going to drive the bootleggers for ever out of this land. It is going to bring clean moving pictures ... clean literature ... break up roadside parking ... enforce the laws ... protect homes.

The Klan was particularly active in the state of Indiana. Robert Coughlan was a Catholic, brought up in the town of Kokomo, Indiana. As a Catholic, he had good reason to be worried by the KKK's strength.

Source 8

R. Coughlan, 'Konklave in Kokomo', in *The Aspirin Age*, 1950.

■ What do you suppose the writer meant by the last sentence in Source 8?

It may be asked why, then, did the town [Kokomo] take so enthusiastically to the Klan? ... Before immigration was finally limited by the quota laws [in the 1920s], many old stock Americans believed they were in danger of being overrun. The 'foreigners were ruining the country'; and so anything 'foreign' was 'un-American' and a menace.

Another important idea in American history was anti-Catholicism because many of the founding fathers had come to America to escape Catholic persecutions in Europe. Once organised in strength, the Klan had an effective weapon in the economic boycott. The anti-Klan merchant saw his trade fade away to the Klan store across the street, where the store window carried a 'TWK' (Trade With Klansmen) sign. It takes great courage to sacrifice a life's work for a principle.

One black newspaper editor in the South wondered why white people did not simply bring blacks to 'white justice':

Source 9

A black newspaper editor from South Carolina, quoted in J. H. Franklin, *From Slavery to Freedom*, 1980.

Why do they lynch Negroes, anyhow? With a white judge, a white jury, white public sentiment, white officers of the law, it is just as impossible for a Negro accused of a crime, or even suspected of a crime, to escape the white man's vengeance or his justice as it would be for a fawn [a young deer] to escape that wanders accidentally into a den of hungry lions.

The Klan 'eklipsed'

Klan membership reached its peak in 1923. In 1925, however, a popular Klan leader in Indiana, David Stephenson, was convicted of the brutal kidnapping, rape and murder of a young woman. He was sentenced to life imprisonment and spent the next 31 years in prison. Within a year, KKK membership fell dramatically from 5 million to 300,000.

Questions

1 Using Sources 4–9, explain why the Ku Klux Klan was so popular in the early 1920s.

2 Many Klansmen wanted American morals and behaviour cleaned up, and laws obeyed (Source 7). How did KKK tactics counter this?

3 Why could the government be accused of encouraging the racist attitudes of groups like the KKK?

4 Why do you think so few KKK members were brought to trial for their crimes?

5 Using Sources 4–9 and the text on the KKK (pages 22–24) explain the reasons for the popularity of the KKK in the South.

1.5 Prohibition and gangsters

Prohibition

In January 1920, the Eighteenth Amendment to the Constitution came into force, *prohibiting* (banning) Americans from selling or making alcohol. Surprisingly, it was not illegal to buy or drink it. The Volstead Act later set down penalties for breaking the new law.

Prohibition, as this policy was known, became law because of pressure from religious organisations like the Anti-Saloon League. It was not a sudden ban, though. The ASL had been campaigning for many years. By 1908, there were already five 'dry' states, where the sale of alcohol was forbidden, in the USA.

The ASL claimed that alcohol was evil and against Christian teaching; it led to drunkenness and violent behaviour. Husbands, they said, wasted their wages on drink and let their families go hungry (Source 1). Businessmen hoped that more sober workers would increase output in their factories.

Prohibition was introduced to strengthen what its supporters claimed was the traditional American way of life: hard work, saving money, and respect for the family and for God. Alcohol, they said, undermined these 'decent' values.

Source 1

Poster produced by the Anti-Saloon League, 1910. It shows a family man handing over his week's wages to the barman. He is described as a 'slave of the saloon' and addicted to drink.

1 Who are the people circled on the right of the picture?

2 Why is the saloon described as 'the poor man's club'?

SLAVES OF THE SALOON

The saloon business cannot exist without slaves. You may smile at that statement, but it is absolutely true. Is not the man who is addicted to the drink habit a slave? There are 1,000,000 such slaves in the United States. They are slaves of the saloon. They go out and work a week or a month, draw their pay, go into the saloon, and hand the saloon keeper their money for something which ruins their own lives. Is not this slavery? Has there ever been in the history of the world a worse system of slavery? It is quite natural, of course, that the slaveholder should not care to liberate these slaves.—*Richmond P. Hobson.*

A woman entered a barroom, and advanced quietly to her husband, who sat drinking with three other men. "Thinkin' ye'l' too busy to come home to supper, Jack, I've fetched it to you here."
And she departed. The man laughed awkwardly. He invited his friends to share the meal with him. Then he removed the cover from the dish. The dish was empty. It contained a slip of paper that said: "I hope you will enjoy your supper. It is the same your wife and children have at home."—*Chicago Chronicle.*

The liquor traffic, like the slave trade or piracy, cannot be mended, and therefore must be actually ended.—*Joseph Cook.*

[A] A poster produced by the Anti-Saloon League, 1910

> Bolshevism flourishes in wet soil. Failure to enforce prohibition in Russian was followed by Bolshevism.
>
> Failure to enforce Prohibition HERE will encourage disrespect for law and INVITE INDUSTRIAL DISASTER.
>
> Radical and Bolshevist outbreaks are practically unknown in states where Prohibition has been in effect for years. Bolshevism live on booze.

[B] From a poster displayed by the Nashville Tennessee chapter of the Anti-Saloon league

Source 2

Anti-Saloon League poster, 1922. There is a reference to patriotism in the caption. This is probably a comment on the fact that many beer-making companies were owned by Americans of German descent, and the United States had fought Germany in the First World War. Drinking beer was therefore seen as unpatriotic and immoral.

1 Who are seen as the 'innocent victims' of alcohol in these two posters (Sources 1 and 2)?

2 How do these posters help to explain why the campaign to outlaw the sale of alcohol was successful?

The OVERSHADOWING CURSE

THE LEGALIZED SALOON

HAS SHE A FAIR CHANCE?

"Our religion demands that every child should have a fair chance for citizenship in the coming Kingdom. Our patriotism demands a saloonless country and a stainless flag."—P. A. Baker, General Superintendent Anti-Saloon League of America.

Prohibition was not so popular in the Northern States. The Southern and Midwestern States, though, were more conservative. They supported Prohibition more enthusiastically because they thought it strengthened the family values they believed in. It was not long, however, before organised crime saw an opportunity to make money from Prohibition.

Public enemy number one: Al Capone

Prohibition was supposed to stop the liquor trade and crime in towns and cities. It failed in this aim. Americans did not stop drinking, and crime continued to flourish. In fact, in some places, Prohibition had the very opposite effect. Some cities such as Chicago became even more corrupt. Illegal drinking became a very popular pastime among many people.

There were a number of ways of getting round the law. 'Bootleggers' sold redistilled industrial alcohol; 'moonshiners' made their own home brews; rum-runners smuggled liquor into the USA from other countries; and hijackers stole alcohol-laden boats, cars and lorries from the bootleggers and rum-runners.

Al Capone was probably the most famous of the bootleggers – those who provided illegal alcohol in 'speakeasies' (places where alcohol was sold against the law). Capone made as much as $100 million a year from his criminal activities, which included illegal gambling and prostitution rackets.

Brutal murder also featured prominently among Capone's activities. On St Valentine's Day in 1929, seven members of the rival Bugs Moran gang were machine-gunned to death by some of Capone's gangsters.

This massacre shocked a public which was not used to gang warfare on such a big scale. The war was over which gang would control the profitable alcohol and prostitution rackets of Chicago. The fact that Capone's men were dressed as policemen made the crime seem even more wicked.

Gangsters were usually careful to avoid harming members of the public. When eight cars of the O'Bannion gang machine-gunned Capone's headquarters, the gangsters in the first car fired blanks to scare away passers-by so they would not be hit by the guns of the other seven cars! Nevertheless, some supporters of Prohibition changed their minds when they saw how it encouraged gangsters, and how criminals like Capone were seen by some people as popular heroes.

Source 3

The massacre of seven members of the Bugs Moran gang by Capone's men, 1929.

Prohibition undermined respect for the law and led to an increase in police corruption, as gangsters bribed policemen and politicians to turn a blind eye to their activities. Needless to say, the price of alcohol soared now it was more difficult to find. Whisky, which cost $4 a gallon before Prohibition, fetched $24 in 1926.

Did Prohibition actually cause the rise of gangsterism? Source 4 suggests that it certainly played a part.

Source 4

F. L. Allen, *Only Yesterday*, 1931. Allen, a well-known journalist, wrote this book as a kind of 'instant history'.

There were over 500 gang murders in all [in the 1920s]. Few of the murderers were ever caught; careful planning, money ... the intimidation of witnesses .... How and why could such a thing happen?

To say that Prohibition ... caused the rise of the gangs to lawless power would be altogether too easy an explanation. There were other causes: the automobile which made escape easy ... the murderous traditions of the Mafia, imported by Sicilian gangsters ....

Yet it is ironically true, nonetheless, that the outburst of corruption and crime in Chicago in the 1920s was immediately caused by the attempt to ban the temptations of alcohol from the American home.

Why was Prohibition a failure?

Prohibition was introduced in 1920 to strengthen what its supporters claimed was the traditional American way of life. It continued until 1933. Despite the efforts of officials, Prohibition was very hard to enforce.

People found many ingenious ways of dodging the laws. Hip flasks were first widely used during Prohibition (Source 5).

Source 5

A woman hiding a flask of liquor in her garter. As hemlines rose to knee-length during the 1920s, it became increasingly tricky for women to hide alcohol in this way!

Opponents of Prohibition claimed that the law was unpopular and could not be enforced. At first, the Federal Government created 1,520 prohibition agents to try to enforce the law. This number increased to 2,836 by 1930. But the agents faced an impossible task, with about 29,000 kilometres of coastline to patrol, and a population of 125 million to police (Source 6).

Source 6

Map of the United States and its neighbouring countries. Alcohol was banned in the USA but not in Canada, Mexico or the Caribbean islands.

1 Why do you think it was so hard for prohibition agents to stop the illegal smuggling of alcohol?

2 Where might alcohol have been smuggled from?

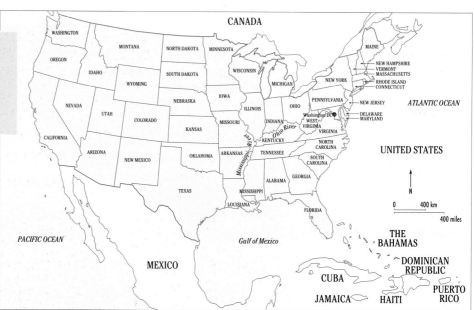

Gangsters who broke the prohibition laws were often not seen by the public as criminals, and this undermined respect for the law as a whole. A modern historian suggests that the public was not especially worried about gangland killings:

Source 7

H. S. Nelli, *The Business of Crime*, 1976.

For all those involved, breaking the law on Prohibition was more acceptable to the public, as well as 'cleaner', than prostitution or drug trafficking. Much of the general public accepted and approved of law-breaking when it involved the manufacture of liquor and beer. Even the murder and maiming of rival gang members ... seemed, to many Americans, to be a modern version of the Old West shoot-out. Such events caused remarkably little anger or concern.

Al Capone defended his 'business' activities as a supplier of illegal alcohol in this way:

Source 8

Al Capone speaking to a journalist in 1931.

If people didn't want beer and wouldn't drink it, a fellow would be crazy going round trying to sell it. I help the public. You can't cure thirst by law. They call me a bootlegger. Yes, it's bootleg while it's on the trucks, but when your host hands it to you on a silver plate it's hospitality.

The role of the film industry in this issue is unclear. The cinema was very popular in the United States and had an important influence on people's attitudes. In the scene below from the film *The Roaring Twenties*, actor James Cagney plays a First World War veteran. In the film, he is driven by poverty into crime. The message of 'Crime does not pay' had to come across in the film, but Cagney is shown here dying in a romantic pose.

Source 9

Scene from the film *The Roaring Twenties*, 1939.

Finally, a journalist gives his views on Prohibition, which he sums up as 'an awful flop':

Source 10

Franklin Adams, a journalist, wrote this amusing comment on Prohibition in 1931. His tone is best described as *ironic* since the reasons he gives for liking Prohibition are not the ones intended by its supporters.

Prohibition is an awful flop.
We like it.
It can't stop what it's meant to stop.
We like it.
It's left a trail of graft and slime,
It's filled our land with vice and crime.
It don't prohibit worth a dime,
Nevertheless, we're for it.

Questions

1 What evidence is there in Sources 7–10 that the public often approved of gangsters?

2 Is the point of view of Al Capone (Source 8) supported by any of the other sources? Explain your answer.

3 Source 10 says that prohibition left 'a trail of graft and slime'.
a What is graft? What do you think Adams meant by slime?
b Why might Prohibition have encouraged this?

4 Use Sources 6–10 and the accompanying text to answer this question: Why was Prohibition a failure?

1.6 Review activity

Why was the USA so racially divided in the 1920s?

This chart looks at reasons why the United States was so racially divided in the period after the First World War. Which reasons were the most important?

Reason for racial division	Effect on racial attitudes	The three most important reasons (with explanation)	Reasons X and Y worked together in making the USA more racially divided because ...
1 The effects of the American Civil War (1861–1865)	The Civil War, Southerners believed, ruined the economy and way of life of the South, and made the South dependent on the North. Some Southerners held black people responsible for the war.	This was very important because it led many Southerners to hate black people and to seek revenge against them for 'causing' the war which had 'ruined' the South.	
2 The legacy (effects) of slavery			
3 Religious differences between Protestants and Catholics			
4 Government immigration policy			
5 The growth of the KKK			
6 Attitudes of the police and the law courts			
7 The 'Red Scare' of the 1920s			

1 Copy the above chart leaving equal amounts of space for each box.

2 First fill in Column 2 to show how each of the reasons in Column 1 affected racial attitudes in the 1920s. (One of these has been done for you.)

3 Now complete Column 3. Choose three of the most important reasons. Explain why you think they were most important in creating this racial division. (One has been done as an example, but you can choose three different ones if you wish.)

4 In Column 4, show how at least two of these reasons worked together in making race relations worse in the USA in the 1920s. What, for example, might be the links between the activities of the KKK and the 'Red Scare' of the 1920s?

Unit 2 · The 1930s: years of gloom

Source 1

A poverty-stricken sharecropper's (tenant farmer's) family in the 1930s.

■ What signs are there in this photograph that the family is poor?

At the end of the 1920s the United States went into a deep economic slump – the Great Depression. The Depression had a terrible effect on the American people. It threw at least 12 million out of work, forcing several million into lives of hunger, homelessness and despair. This Unit looks at how the Depression affected Americans during the 1930s and examines the government's attempts to overcome it. We begin by investigating the causes of this economic disaster.

2.1 From boom to gloom

The year 1929 is usually taken as the time when the economic collapse began, but things were already going wrong before then. Farmers were in difficulties well before 1929. Many farmers had already lost their farms. In 1929 the average annual income of a South Carolina farmer was $1,550 – just $50 a year above the 'poverty line'.

The Wall Street Crash

In October 1929, the US stock market – Wall Street – crashed. In just a few days, people all over the country were ruined. Why were so many people affected?

Before the Crash, the *New York Times* share index, which measured the strength of the share market, had risen dramatically from 106 in 1924 to 542 in 1929. This meant that the value of shares had risen five times. Shares had risen in value because investors had driven up the prices by buying so many. It seemed a foolproof way to make money. Shares in the

Radio Corporation of America, for example, cost $85 each in early 1928; by September 1929 they were worth $505 each – nearly six times as much.

Many people who did not have the cash to buy shares in full borrowed money from a bank or broker. This was called 'buying on the margin'. After all, the money borrowed could always be paid back from the profit made when the shares were sold.

However, in September 1929 some shrewd investors realised that sooner or later the stock market would stop rising, and they began to sell their shares. Other investors grew nervous and copied them. In October the trickle of sellers became a torrent as millions of shares were sold. On Black Thursday – 24 October – 13 million were sold in a single day.

As a result, share prices collapsed. Those people who had borrowed to buy their now almost worthless shares were ruined. The shares of Union Cigar, for example, fell from $113 to just $4 in one day. The president of the company jumped to his death from the ledge of a New York hotel. Many were forced to sell their homes to pay back what they had borrowed. Others withdrew their savings from banks to pay back what they owed and this caused some banks to fail. By the end of 1932, 22 per cent of banks had gone out of business, losing their customers' savings in the process.

Source 2

The cartoonist, John McCutcheon, won a prize for this cartoon in 1932. The man on the bench has lost all his savings in a bank which has gone out of business.

■ Do you think the cartoonist is sympathetic or hostile to the man in the picture? Explain your answer.

Over-production

Spectacular as it was, the Wall Street Crash was not the real *cause* of the Great Depression – it simply made the economic problems worse. One basic reason for the slump was *over-production*. During the prosperous 1920s, consumers had been keen to buy all sorts of goods – especially the newly mass-produced ones such as vacuum cleaners, refrigerators and cars. By the end of the 1920s, though, consumers had bought all the goods they wanted or could afford. Companies were forced to cut back on production and cut prices to tempt buyers. By the summer of 1929, warehouses began to fill with unsold goods. Workers were laid off and profits began to fall.

Whilst those who could afford consumer goods had already got them, others were scratching a living and could not afford them. In 1929, 43 per cent of families earned less than $1,500 a year. They were struggling during the so-called 'boom' years of the Twenties; they never had been able to afford the feast of goods being turned out by factories across America.

Companies could always try selling abroad those goods Americans could not buy at home – in theory. However, the Fordney–McCumber tariff of 1922, which taxed foreign goods imported into America, led the governments of other countries to impose taxes on US goods in return, to make them more expensive in their countries. So this outlet for surplus goods was not available.

Source 3

The crisis of over-production. It was a vicious downward spiral leading to unemployment and bankruptcy. Unemployment rose from 1.5 million in 1929 to 4.3 million in 1930. Those who still had jobs were afraid of losing them and decided to save what they could rather than spend. This meant that even fewer goods were sold.

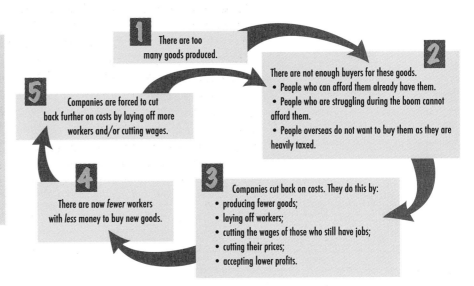

1 There are too many goods produced.

2 There are not enough buyers for these goods.
• People who can afford them already have them.
• People who are struggling during the boom cannot afford them.
• People overseas do not want to buy them as they are heavily taxed.

3 Companies cut back on costs. They do this by:
• producing fewer goods;
• laying off workers;
• cutting the wages of those who still have jobs;
• cutting their prices;
• accepting lower profits.

4 There are now *fewer* workers with *less* money to buy new goods.

5 Companies are forced to cut back further on costs by laying off more workers and/or cutting wages.

Declining industries

Some traditional industries were already in decline. The coal industry, for example, could not compete with newer forms of energy like oil, electricity and gas. These sources of energy now supplied more than half of America's energy needs. During the 1920s, many coal mines were shut down and miners lost their jobs.

The textile industry was also in trouble before the Depression. Cotton was especially badly hit. This was partly because women's fashions now required much less material. It has been estimated that it took 19 metres of material to dress a woman in 1913, but only 7 metres in 1928. Artificial fibres like rayon – a new material developed in the 1920s – were also replacing cotton in popularity.

Source 4

A woman in short skirt and turned-down stockings, powdering her knees. The 1920s fashion of short skirts exposed knees for the first time. Before the war, skirts had reached down to women's ankles.

■ Why was this new fashion bad for the textile industry?

The role of government

Could the government have done more to prevent the Depression? Herbert Hoover was President from 1928. As a Republican, he did not believe that governments should interfere with the running of the economy. He thought that the Depression would soon end and the economy would pick up again. He did not believe that the government should spend money to help the unemployed and the poor. They would have to help themselves.

What was the main cause of the Depression?

Historians and economists do not agree on what caused the Great Depression. Some historians say that over-production was the main cause. Others point to different causes, or stress that there was a combination of causes.

Source 5

A different interpretation: under-demand. This cartoon is from a cartoon history of the United States, published in 1991. The cartoonist makes it clear that historians do not always agree on the causes of events like the Depression.

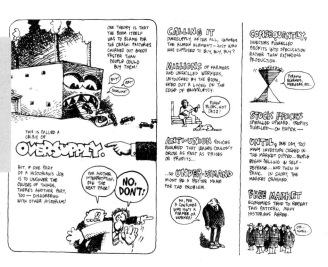

Questions

1 Why were workers being laid off towards the end of the 1920s?

2 Even though the Wall Street Crash was not a major cause of the Depression, can you suggest any ways in which it made the Depression worse?

3 Look carefully at Source 5.
   a Which two different interpretations of the Depression does the cartoonist describe?
   b What two reasons for under-demand does he give?
   c The cartoonist thinks that *under-demand* was the real cause of the Depression. Does this mean that the other interpretation, *over-supply*, is wrong?

2.2 The effects of the Depression

Hard times

Many Americans were devastated by the Depression. Starvation was a real threat. In Chicago, for example, desperate women would pick over rubbish for scraps of food for the family. Millions of workers were laid off work. As well as the despair of looking in vain for another job, the unemployed and their families had to contend with hunger, weariness and the fear of homelessness.

Many were forced to give up their homes because they could not pay their rent or mortgage. Impoverished families built themselves slum homes of canvas and wood in shanties known as 'Hoovervilles' – a bitter reference to the President who was apparently doing so little to help them.

Needy people were dependent on private charity. Without any unemployment benefit to help them, the unemployed were forced to queue for charity hand-outs in bread lines – some of them 10,000 people long.

Source 1

Unemployed people queuing in New York for free food, 1930. Bread lines and soup kitchens became a familiar sight in cities during the Depression.

Hoover and 'rugged individualism'

It was soon clear that private charity was unable to deal with a crisis on this scale. Charities quickly ran out of funds. By 1932, the Red Cross, for example, could only give 75 cents a week to each needy family. However, Herbert Hoover, who became President in 1928, did not believe that the state should organise work, food and shelter for the needy. Many Republicans shared this view.

Hoover's response to the crisis was to sit it out, confident that the economy would soon recover on its own. 'Prosperity is just around the corner,' he told the public. He reminded the people that prosperity would only happen if businesses were not told what to do by the government. Hoover believed strongly in the 'American spirit' – that of 'rugged individuals' who sorted out their own problems without the government's interference.

Source 2

How many people were unemployed?

Date	Number of people unemployed (in millions)
1929	1.5
1930	5
1931	9
1932	13

It was also an important part of 'rugged individualism' that economic freedom went hand in hand with political freedom. Hoover believed that once governments started telling businesses how to run their affairs, the next thing would be that people would be told what to think.

His beliefs did not mean that Hoover did nothing to tackle the Depression. Nor did they mean that he did not care about the terrible plight of so many people. He created several agencies to deal with poverty, such as the President's Organisation for Unemployment Relief (POUR). However, POUR did not spend government money, but only money donated to it to help the unemployed. Eventually, Hoover was persuaded that the government had to do something, and in late 1931 he set up the Reconstruction Finance Corporation. The RFC lent money from the Federal Government to help out troubled banks and businesses. But it was now too little and too late.

How did the Depression affect the American people?

There is a great deal of evidence available from the Depression. Thousands of letters, photographs, interviews and personal stories tell of the misery and despair of unemployment, homelessness, and life on low wages. However, there is also evidence which suggests that many Americans were not so badly affected by the Depression. The sources which follow reflect these different experiences.

Letters written by unemployed people are an important source of evidence. About 15 million Americans wrote to Franklin D. Roosevelt, Hoover's successor, during his presidency. Some were critical of his policies, but most approved. Many asked for money or a job to help them out of their financial problems. Source 3 is typical.

Source 3

A letter to President Roosevelt, 1934. Note that the original spelling and punctuation in the letters (Sources 3, 4 and 7) has been kept.

Lawndale, California
Feb. 1-1934

Most Honourable President:
... I am a mother of seven children, and utterly heart broken, in that they are hungry, have only 65 cents in money. The father is in L.A. trying to find something to do, – all provisions gone – at this writing – no meat, milk – sugar – in fact, about enough flour for bread two meals – and thats all ....

O, what a burden and how helpless I am, how proud I am of my children, and how dark a future under this condition.

Their father is 62 yrs, old – a preacher a good carpenter – a saw-filer – but Industry won't hire a man his age ... O surely there's a place for us in this world ... I humbly pray God's divine blessing on you, for you have tried in every way to help the people.

Very Sincerely,
Mrs I.H.

Not all the letters sent to the White House went to the President. Some were addressed to his wife, Eleanor Roosevelt. Not all the letters came from families of unemployed working class people, either. The middle classes were hit badly, too, as this letter from an unemployed surveyor makes clear:

Source 4

Extract from a letter written by a surveyor's wife to Mrs Roosevelt in June 1934.

■ Why do you think this woman might have written to Mrs Roosevelt, rather than the President?

.... Then came the Depression. My work [in the County Court House] has continued and my salary alone has just been sufficient to make our monthly payments on the house and keep our bills paid. But ... my husband [a surveyor] has not had work since August 1932.

My salary could continue to keep us going, but – I am going to have a baby ... now that it has happened, I won't give it up! I'm willing to undergo any hardship for myself and I can get a leave of absence for a year. But can't you, won't you do something so my husband can have a job, at least during that year?

As I said before, if it were only ourselves, or if there were something we could do about it, we would never ask for help. We have always stood on our own two feet and been proud and happy. But you are a mother and you'll understand this crisis ....

Very sincerely yours

Mrs M.H.A.

Tape-recorded interviews are a major source of evidence about the Depression. Studs Terkel, an American writer who lived through the Depression, collected hundreds of interviews with other survivors and published them in his book *Hard Times*. Source 5 is part of an interview with a psychiatrist, Dr Rossman, who treated people during the Depression.

Source 5

Interview by Studs Terkel, quoted in *Hard Times*, 1970.

Dr Rossman: You wouldn't know a depression was going on. Except that people were complaining that they didn't have any jobs ... But on the whole – don't forget that the highest unemployment was less than 20 per cent.

Terkel: Your patients, then, weren't really affected?

Dr Rossman: Not very much. They paid fairly reasonable fees. I just came across a handbook that I had between 1931 and 1934, and, by God, I was in those days making $2,000 a month, which was a hell of a lot of money ....

Source 6 is one of Hank Oettinger's memories of the Depression. He was interviewed by Studs Terkel, too. Oettinger was a printworker before losing his job in the Depression. Here he remembers seeing unemployed workers marching in protest through the streets:

Source 6

Interview by Studs Terkel, quoted in *Hard Times*, 1970.

I remember seeing a hunger march to City Hall. It was a very cold, bitter day. My boss was looking out the window with me. I didn't know what the hell it was. He says, 'They ought to lock the bastards up.'

The issue of race did not disappear during the Depression. Racism against black people was especially strong in states of the Deep South. The poverty of many whites led some to turn against blacks even more, as this letter makes clear:

Source 7

A letter to President Roosevelt, July 1935. It was written by a white woman from Georgia. She did not give her name.

dear Sur as you are the president of our state it looks like you could do something to help out the poor white people the negroes can get work where the poor white man canot ... The negroes are in the post offices getting $1,000 dollars a month and white families suffering and it is not write .... there is a negro working in the post office and white men cant get a job to feed his family ... and negroes being worked ever where instead of white men it don't look that it is rite and is not rite and lay off white men ....

Questions

1 What do Dr Rossman in Source 5 and Hank Oettinger's boss in Source 6 have in common?

2 What do these sources (2–7) suggest about how the Depression affected different Americans?

2.3 A New Deal for Americans

Source 1

Cartoon of Roosevelt taking over from Hoover as President, 1933.

New president, new direction, new deal

The 1932 presidential election was won easily by the Democratic Party candidate, Franklin Delano Roosevelt. The voters turned their backs on twelve years of government by Republican presidents. In particular, they rejected Hoover's empty promises and his refusal to tackle seriously the effects of the Depression.

Roosevelt caught the mood of the voters with his promise of a 'New Deal' for the American people: the government would create jobs by *spending* money in a variety of public work schemes such as building dams. Once these workers were earning wages, Roosevelt argued, they could start buying goods, and firms would begin hiring new workers. These workers in turn would spend money, and so on.

This was a radical new approach: never before had the Federal Government played such an important part in the economy. Large public works schemes were unheard of in the USA before the 1930s.

How does the cartoonist get across his disapproval of Hoover's policies?

The Federal Government introduced numerous laws, set up new government organisations, and spent billions of dollars to help businesses, bankers, workers, the unemployed, and those in debt. This New Deal, as Roosevelt called it, brought relief to the needy, promoted recovery, and reformed the economy.

Roosevelt believed that through public works, the unemployed would regain their self-respect and their faith in democracy. He warned that 'People who are hungry and are out of a job are the stuff of which dictatorships are made.'

The First New Deal

The First New Deal was a series of policies between 1933 and 1935, intended to get the economy working again.

The first major problem facing Roosevelt was the collapse of some 1,500 banks by the end of 1932. The public had to be convinced that their money was safe and that they should stop withdrawing their savings from the banks, since this only made more of them go bankrupt.

Roosevelt took over as President in March 1933 and the first act he introduced was the *Emergency Banking Act*. All banks were closed for ten days and only those approved by the Federal Government were allowed to reopen. Roosevelt skilfully used the radio in a series of 'fireside chats' to explain his policies. The President explained that it was safer to 'keep your money in a reopened bank than under the mattress'. It worked. When the banks reopened, people began investing their savings in them again.

Relief of people's distress was an urgent priority too. *The Federal Emergency Relief Act* provided $500 million of benefits to the states for the unemployed and the poor, provided they added money of their own as well. This was to be only a temporary measure, as Roosevelt was anxious that the unemployed should be found useful work to do rather than just given government 'hand-outs'.

Young men aged 18–25 also found work through the *Civilian Conservation Corps* in camps throughout America. They planted trees to stop soil erosion, and strengthened river banks to prevent flooding. A small monthly payment was made to each worker's family. By the end of the 1930s, 2.75 million men (and a small number of women) had served in the CCC.

Finally, people could now celebrate their more hopeful future with a drink, since Roosevelt also abolished Prohibition in 1933.

Farmers: produce less!

The most controversial of Roosevelt's New Deal policies was the *Agricultural Adjustment Act* (AAA) of 1933. Farming had been depressed since the mid 1920s because of falling prices caused by over-production. In some places, selling a wagon-load of oats earned farmers less than it cost to buy a pair of shoes. Wheat in Montana was left to rot in the fields, because it did not pay to shift the harvest.

Roosevelt wanted farmers to produce *fewer* crops, such as corn and cotton, and less meat. In this way prices would rise and farmers could begin to sell at a profit again. To make up for the loss of income while they were producing less, farmers were given money by the government. The

AAA also backed a programme to plough the bumper cotton crop of 1933 back into the ground, and to slaughter 6 million pigs. This, too, was meant to prevent over-production. The government had thus launched a very controversial policy to force up food prices and destroy crops at a time when millions in the cities were going hungry.

Another agency set up in 1933 to help farmers and others was the *Tennessee Valley Authority* (TVA). Farmland in the Tennessee Valley had become very poor because of over-cultivation, flooding and soil erosion. Only one farm in fifty had electricity and half its population of 2.5 million was living below the poverty line. The TVA was an ambitious scheme intended to provide cheap electricity, stop floods, and make the soil fertile again. Twenty dams were built to generate electricity, and millions of trees planted to stop further soil erosion. The experiment worked. By 1943, for example, 80 per cent of the valley farms had transferred from kerosene lamps to electricity.

Source 2

The Tennessee Valley Authority. The Tennessee Valley was a vast area of over 60,000 square kilometres, spanning seven different states (an area four-fifths the size of England).

The Second New Deal – a good deal for workers

The Second New Deal began in 1935. It was more concerned with protecting the rights of workers and providing some social security benefits. The 1935 *Social Security Act* (SSA) began the first national system of old-age pensions. Employers and workers now paid into a Federal Government pension fund. The Act also provided a plan of unemployment benefits – each state was to work out its own details.

The SSA was not very generous by European standards but it did mark a dramatic change in traditional American attitudes about how much the state should 'interfere' in people's lives. There was much opposition from conservative Republicans who thought the schemes smacked of socialism.

Other agencies, like the *Works Progress Administration* (WPA), employed workers to build schools, hospitals and roads, and even found assignments for writers, artists and photographers (see also page 45). By 1942, 8 million people had been employed through this scheme. The photograph opposite (Source 3) was taken by Dorothea Lange on such an assignment for the WPA. Her photographs seemed to sum up the despair of the millions whose lives were ruined by the Depression.

Source 3

This Mexican farm worker is standing outside his home in California in 1937. He was a migrant worker who moved around in search of temporary work.

1 What signs are there in the photograph that he is poor?

2 Why do you think he still has a car, despite his poverty?

Roosevelt was also anxious to defend the right of workers to join a trade union. Many big industrialists like Henry Ford were fiercely opposed to trade unions, and dismissed any worker who joined one. The *Wagner Act* of 1935 gave every worker the right to join a union. The number of union members rose from 3 million in 1933 to 10 million in 1941. The Act also set up a National Labour Relations Board to punish employers who did not recognise workers' rights.

How successful was the New Deal?

To answer this question, first think about what the New Deal was *aiming* to do. The New Deal tried to bring immediate relief to the desperate millions, and to revive the American economy. Once the government had given the initial boost, the economy was intended to 'spiral' up to prosperity. How successful was it in its aims?

Statistics like those in Sources 4–7 may help to answer this question but remember that statistics are difficult sources to deal with. They can sometimes be presented in ways which change their meaning entirely. For example, why might a supporter of Roosevelt be tempted to leave out the 1938 unemployment figures from Source 4, and use only those from 1933 to 1937?

Source 4 shows how the number of people out of work changed after the New Deal began in 1933.

Source 4

Date	Number of unemployed (in millions)
1933	12.8
1934	11.3
1935	10.6
1936	9.0
1937	7.7
1938	10.4
1939	9.5
1940	8.1
1941	5.6

Source 5 shows the size of America's Gross National Product, or GNP, during this period. GNP is the measurement of how much wealth a country is producing.

Source 5

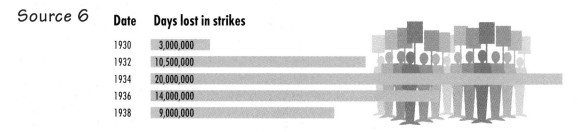

Date	Gross National Product (GNP in $ billions)
1933	56
1934	65
1935	72
1936	83
1937	91
1938	85
1939	91
1940	101
1941	126

Another useful measure of the economy's health is the number of days lost in strikes. This means the number of workers on strike over a number of days. For example, 1,000 workers on strike for 10 days would mean 10,000 days 'lost in strikes'. The figures are often used to show how satisfied workers are with their conditions and pay.

Source 6

Date	Days lost in strikes
1930	3,000,000
1932	10,500,000
1934	20,000,000
1936	14,000,000
1938	9,000,000

A high price for wheat meant that the farmers were more prosperous. What does the following table show?

Source 7

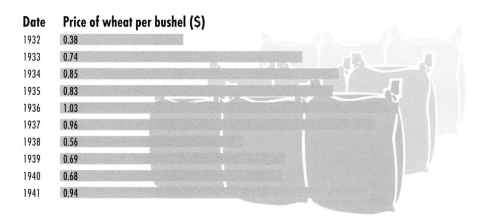

Date	Price of wheat per bushel ($)
1932	0.38
1933	0.74
1934	0.85
1935	0.83
1936	1.03
1937	0.96
1938	0.56
1939	0.69
1940	0.68
1941	0.94

Statistics can only tell part of the story. Many of the 12.8 million unemployed in 1933 had families, which means that as many as 40 million men, women and children may have been affected by unemployment. Nor do the statistics distinguish between black people and white people. Did the New Deal help all Americans equally?

Black people and the New Deal

One area in which Roosevelt was reluctant to intervene was the civil rights of black people. In 1935 a law against lynching was suggested to the President. He refused to support it, however, because he would lose the support of Democratic members of Congress from the South. Their support was vital if Roosevelt's New Deal policies were to become law.

In fact, during the nearly fifteen years that he was President, Roosevelt only passed one civil rights law for black people. In 1941 it became illegal to discriminate against black people in the employment practices of the defence industries. The armed forces remained segregated, though, so that blacks and whites could not serve in the same unit.

The New Deal itself did little for black people, since most black people in work had jobs as unskilled workers, and in this area the New Deal had less impact.

Source 8

A line of black people queuing for government relief, 1937. The poster directly behind them proclaims that America has 'the world's highest standard of living'.

■ What point do you think the photographer was making?

Women in the 1930s

The 1920s had been a decade of experiment and daring for many women (see pages 16–19). Many traditional attitudes which had restricted the lives of women before the war were broken down. But the 1930s were years of hardship and sacrifice. Although the number of women in work actually rose during the Depression to about 25 per cent of women – because they were cheaper to employ than men – their earnings were poor. The average pay for a woman in 1937 was $525, compared to $1,027 for a man. The situation for black women was worse: 40 per cent of black women worked, but for even lower wages than white women.

The New Deal offered little to women. *The National Industrial Recovery Act* of 1933 drew up a series of codes which set minimum wages, prices, and maximum working hours in industry. About a quarter of these codes actually required women to be paid less than men. Only 8,000 women were employed by the Civilian Conservation Corps out of the 2.75 million involved in the scheme.

Women in the home

The home was still the expected focus for the vast majority of women. In this sense their lives were less obviously disrupted by the Depression than the lives of men who were out of work:

Source 9

Extract from R. and H. Lynd, *Middletown in Transition*, 1937, a survey of social and cultural change in an American town in the 1930s.

The men, cut adrift from their usual routine, lost much of their sense of time and dawdled helplessly and dully about the streets; while in the homes the women's world remained largely intact and the round of cooking, house-cleaning, and mending became if anything more absorbing.

■ Why do you think some women might disagree with the suggestion that the Depression affected them less than men?

Source 10

Amelia Earhart from Kansas – an inspiring aviator. In 1937 she set out to fly round the world. Tragically her plane was lost over the Pacific Ocean.

Independent women

In the 1930s, some women emerged as exceptional individuals. In the 1920s most sporting heroes had been men but in the 1930s more women emerged to establish themselves as national sporting figures in tennis, skating and golf. For example, Helen Wills Moody became a great world-class tennis player, whilst Glenna Collett Vare had a distinguished career in golf. Amelia Earhart was the best known of several prominent women aviators. She was the first person to fly solo from Hawaii to the Pacific coast.

Film stars such as Mae West and Greta Garbo played strong, independent characters in the movies. Women were also increasingly shown as single and career–minded, and home-making was no longer seen as the only option for young women. The importance of the cinema should not be underestimated at a time when 60 million Americans (out of a population of 140 million) went to the cinema each week.

Women in politics

Another area where women made some progress in the 1930s was in politics. Only one woman was elected as a senator in the 1930s and only a handful became Congresswomen in each election. However, greater numbers of women were elected to the various state assemblies, and more women found jobs in positions associated with the New Deal.

Eleanor Roosevelt played a major role in encouraging this trend. President Roosevelt appointed the first woman to serve in the government, making Frances Perkins his Secretary of Labour. A woman was also appointed director of the US Mint.

The Depression and the arts

Writers found powerful themes to write about in the Great Depression. Novelists like Erskine Caldwell and James T. Farrell found much to criticise in a system which left so many people in despair and poverty.

The novel which probably best describes the effects of the Depression is John Steinbeck's *The Grapes of Wrath*. The book took America and Britain by storm when it was first published in 1939. Although Steinbeck's story of the desperate search for work of a poor farming family is a bitter one, the Joad family never loses its sense of decency or its hope for a better future. In this way the novel is a symbol of the 'American spirit'.

Source 11

Scene from the film of Steinbeck's novel, *The Grapes of Wrath*, made in 1939. It starred Henry Fonda – an actor who had already made a name for himself portraying the traditional, decent, God-fearing and caring American.

■ Why do you think *The Grapes of Wrath* was such a popular film?

An entirely different response to the Depression came from the 'dream factory' of Hollywood. When 60 million Americans went to the cinema each week, they did not go to be reminded about the hardships of the Depression but to escape from them. Hollywood happily obliged. The Fred Astaire/Ginger Rogers and Busby Berkeley musicals of the 1930s provided romantic escapism. The hugely successful romantic drama of 1938, *Gone with the Wind*, did tell of hardship and suffering – but from the American Civil War era of 70 years earlier.

The *Works Progress Administration* provided temporary employment for out-of-work artists, photographers, writers, musicians and actors. Writers produced guidebooks for all the states across America, discussing their local traditions, history and geography. The New Deal in this way made Americans more aware of their own culture and traditions than they had been before, and gave popular culture a more important place in American life.

Source 12

Dam under construction in a mural by William Gropper, 1930s. He was an artist paid by the Works Progress Administration. The mural shows how the New Deal was putting Americans back to work in useful construction projects.

■ Roosevelt's critics accused him of spending government money on propaganda campaigns to convince Americans that his policies were succeeding. Do you think this was fair?

Interpreting the New Deal

Sources 13 and 14 are secondary sources. Both are taken from school textbooks. They give two different views on Roosevelt and the success of his policies.

Source 13

John Traynor, *Roosevelt's America, 1932–41*, 1987.

recession A period when unemployment rises and factories produce less.

Worried that his government was spending too much money [in 1938], Roosevelt himself took the decision to lay off thousands of workers employed by the Works Progress Administration. During what people called the 'Roosevelt recession'* unemployment soared, so that by 1938 over ten million people were once again without work …. Ironically, it was the war rather than the New Deal which brought prosperity back to America.

Source 14

Bryn O'Callaghan, *An Illustrated History of the USA*, 1990.

To millions of Americans, he [Roosevelt] was the man who had given them jobs and saved their homes and farms. In 1936 they re-elected him by the largest majority of votes in the country's history …. Thirty years later a New York taxi driver still remembered how many Americans felt about Roosevelt in those years: 'Roosevelt?' he said in a television interview. 'He was God in this country.'… Roosevelt taught Americans to look to the government to see that everyone had a fair chance to obtain what he called 'the good things of life'. Many Americans still remember him with respect and affection.

Questions

1 How could a supporter of the New Deal use the statistics in Sources 4–7 to show that it was a success?

2 What evidence is there in Sources 4–7 to support the claim of Source 13 that there was a recession in 1938?

3 Do you agree with Source 14 that the government under Roosevelt saw to it that 'everyone had a fair chance to obtain "the good things of life"'? Explain your answer.

4 Using Sources 4–7 and the accompanying text, explain which source – 13 or 14 – most accurately sums up the New Deal for you.

2.4 Opponents of the New Deal

Roosevelt faced opposition from a variety of groups and organisations. He was criticised by some for interfering too much with business, and by others for not doing enough to end the Depression. Some opposed him because they believed that the Federal Government was taking too much power from the governments of the individual states, and spending taxpayers' money too freely. This issue of *states' rights* is more easily understood if one first explains how the American political system works.

How the American political system works

The United States is a *federal republic*. 'Federal' means that a country is united and has a national government. But it also allows for regions, or states, to have their own powers, and to make their own state laws in certain things. In the USA, many important powers are not in the hands of the Federal Government, but in the hands of the 50 states. 'Republic' means that there is no hereditary monarch (king or queen). Instead there is a President, and he (or she) is elected periodically.

Laws in America are passed by *Congress*. This is the equivalent of Britain's Parliament. Congress is made up of two elected groups of people: *Senators* who meet in the *Senate*; and *Congressmen* and *women* who meet in the *House of Representatives*. Congress is a powerful body. Once it has passed a law, it is the job of the President, as leader of the Federal Government, to put it into effect.

The President chooses his own advisers to help him run the Federal Government, and he puts forward his policies to Congress for its approval. Quite often, Congress rejects these policies, making the President's job very difficult. Problems can also arise from the fact that it is possible for the President to belong to one political party (Republican or Democrat), and for Congress to be led by the other party.

The diagram below shows how the American political system works:

Source 1

The American political system. Note that the diagram applies only to the Federal Government. Individual states can act independently in many matters.

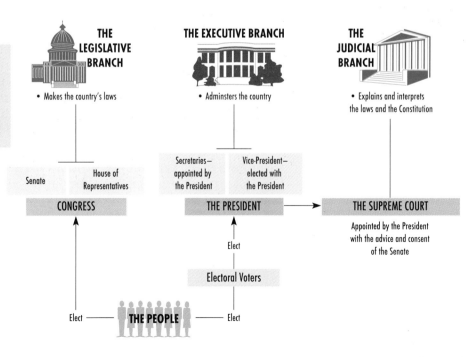

THE LEGISLATIVE BRANCH
• Makes the country's laws

THE EXECUTIVE BRANCH
• Adminsters the country

THE JUDICIAL BRANCH
• Explains and interprets the laws and the Constitution

Senate | House of Representatives
CONGRESS

Secretaries— appointed by the President | Vice-President— elected with the President
THE PRESIDENT

THE SUPREME COURT
Appointed by the President with the advice and consent of the Senate

Electoral Voters

Elect — THE PEOPLE — Elect

The American Constitution was designed to work on the principle of 'checks and balances'. This means that Americans wanted to limit or 'check' the power of the presidency by 'balancing' it with the Supreme Court and Congress. Source 2 shows the 'balanced' powers of the President, the Supreme Court and Congress:

Source 2

The separation of powers.

■ How does this diagram show how the powers of the President are checked by the other two bodies?

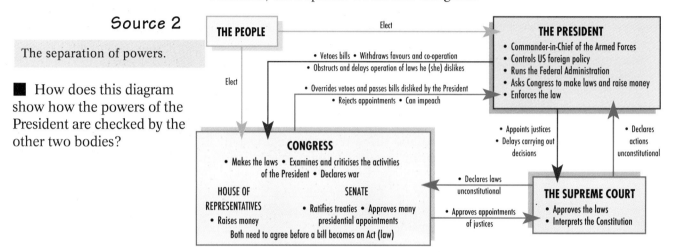

The issue of states' rights

The Federal Government makes decisions on issues which affect the whole country, such as whether to go to war or not, and what taxes the people should pay. But individual states have quite a lot of power, too. For example, each state can make its own decision about whether to have the death penalty, or whether alcoholic drinks should be sold inside the state borders.

The individual states often clash with the Federal Government because they believe that the right of the states to make their own laws is being taken over by the Federal Government. This is what is meant by *states' rights*.

During the New Deal, campaigners for states' rights objected to schemes like the TVA (see page 40) which forced them to co-operate in the Federal Government's plan to build dams across seven states.

Opposition from the Supreme Court

Perhaps Roosevelt's most serious opposition came from the Supreme Court. The Supreme Court consists of nine judges, appointed for life, whose task is to make sure laws passed by Congress do not break the Constitution. The Supreme Court in 1935 and 1936 decided that several of Roosevelt's New Deal laws were unconstitutional – that is, they broke the laws of the Constitution. This meant they were illegal.

After his overwhelming victory in the 1936 presidential election (when he won 61 per cent of the votes), Roosevelt decided that public opinion was behind his New Deal. So he threatened to retire those judges in the Supreme Court over the age of 70 and replace them with younger judges. Needless to say, these new judges would be Roosevelt supporters. However, this threat caused a lot of opposition and the President abandoned it. Fortunately for Roosevelt, some judges retired anyway and the Supreme Court stopped opposing his policies.

Opposition from rich businessmen

Wealthy business organisations, such as the American Liberty League, opposed Roosevelt. They did not like the way the New Deal 'interfered' with businesses and gave support to workers. The League was formed by a group of conservative businessmen that included Al Smith and John Davis, two previous Democratic presidential candidates – but its main support came from rich enemies of Roosevelt who despised him because, although a rich man himself, he had chosen to help the poor.

'Every man a king but no man wears a crown'

A more serious threat came from the Senator for Louisiana, Huey Long. Long criticised Roosevelt for *not doing enough* to end poverty and the Depression. He called for heavy taxation of the rich and the total confiscation of all fortunes over $5 million. His 'Share Our Wealth' scheme, Long claimed, would give each American family $6,000 to spend. This would boost the economy and pull it out of the Depression. His book, *Every Man a King*, published in 1933, promised economic security for all.

'Share Our Wealth' clubs sprang up all over America and claimed a membership of 7.5 million. Long, as Governor of Louisiana, was also a ruthless politician who would not tolerate any opposition, and he made many enemies. One of the men he had ruined, a doctor, took his revenge in 1935. Long's bodyguards fired 61 bullets into the doctor, but not before he had been able to fire the one shot which killed Huey Long.

How did opponents react to the New Deal?

Roosevelt's policies were popular with the unemployed and working class people of the United States. Rich Americans tended to have a different view. Some believed that the President was wasting taxpayers' money; others that he was harming businesses with policies which protected workers' interests and not those of the employers.

The cartoons in Sources 3–6 show various hostile views of the New Deal:

Source 3

Cartoon of 1936 shows two wealthy businessmen crying over the effects of the New Deal.

■ What do the newspaper headlines in the background suggest?

Cartoon from the *Washington Post*, 1936, shows Harry Hopkins, the man in charge of the New Deal's welfare policies.

Source 4

Source 5

Cartoon from *St Columbus Despatch*, 1930s. Roosevelt is 'pump-priming' the economy – pumping government money into the economy in an effort to get it started up again.

Source 6

The children in this cartoon belong to a well-off family, judging by the house in the background.

"Mother Wilfred wrote a bad word!"

Questions

1 Why is the cartoonist in Source 3 poking fun at the two businessmen?

2 Why is the cartoonist in Source 4 opposed to Roosevelt's New Deal?

3 How does the cartoonist in Source 5 show (i) that Roosevelt's efforts are failing; (ii) that the New Deal is a waste of taxpayers' money?

4 **a** Why might a rich family like the one in Source 6 consider 'Roosevelt' to be a 'bad' word?

  b What does the cartoon suggest about Roosevelt's popularity among the rich in the 1930s?

5 Suggest why Sources 3 and 6 could be seen as different from Sources 4 and 5 in the way they treat Roosevelt.

2.5 Review activity

Who supported the New Deal?

This chart looks at how Americans reacted to the New Deal, and why they reacted as they did.

Group	Supporters or opponents?	Reason
1 Unemployed workers		
2 Industrial workers		
3 Black workers	Probably supporters, but largely unaffected.	The New Deal mostly benefited skilled and unionised workers; most black workers were neither of these.
4 States' rights supporters		
5 The Supreme Court		
6 Employers (bosses)		
7 Women		

1 Copy the chart above.

2 Fill in Column 2, saying whether the group listed in Column 1 supported the New Deal or not.

3 Now give the reason for your answer in Column 3. (One group has already been filled in for you.)

Unit 3 · The USA at war

In 1941, the United States was forced to drop its usual policy of isolationism and went to war against Germany, Italy and Japan. A Russian revolutionary, Leon Trotsky, described war as the 'locomotive of history'. He meant by this that war increased the speed at which change took place. Was this true of the USA?

This unit shows how the Second World War affected the lives and attitudes of Americans, and invites you to decide how far the war changed them. To begin with we look at how the USA gradually moved away from isolationism, and then we see how the war affected the economy, black people and women.

3.1 From isolation to world war

Neutrality in the 1930s

Roosevelt largely stuck to America's policy of isolationism during the 1930s. As war clouds gathered in Europe and Asia, he was keen to keep America out of conflicts in other continents, while protecting US interests in Central and South America. Such policies were supported by the American public. The *Neutrality Act* of 1936 stopped loans to countries at war. The 1937 *Neutrality Act* forbade the sale of weapons to countries at war.

Source 1

The storm in the Pacific: Japanese expansion in the 1930s.

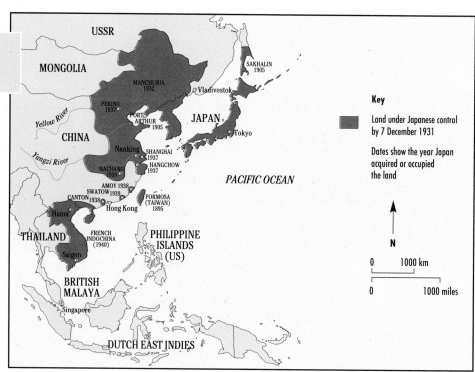

American determination to steer clear of European problems also meant that the USA refused to increase the number of immigrants allowed into the country. This stood at 150,000 a year. In 1933 Adolf Hitler came to power in Germany. Thousands of Jews trying to escape from Nazi persecution in the 1930s were turned away by the United States. (It should be pointed out, though, that Jews trying to flee to other countries, such as Britain, were not treated any better.)

Events in Asia created problems for Roosevelt. In 1931 the Japanese invaded Manchuria, and China itself in 1937. This action broke several treaties which the USA and Japan had signed, as well as Japan's pledge as a member of the League of Nations. China asked the USA and the League to help, but neither was willing. The United States was now unable to trade with Japanese-controlled China, but Congress still refused to take any measures against Japan. Americans, still struggling with the effects of the Depression, were in no mood to get involved in conflicts between peoples in distant countries.

Why did the United States end its isolationism?

The outbreak of war in Europe led to a gradual weakening of isolationism in the USA. Americans began to wake up to the threat that Nazi Germany and Fascism posed to their belief in world peace and democracy.

In 1940, Americans were shocked when France fell to the Nazis. Roosevelt and the 'internationalists' believed that Britain must now be helped to ensure its survival, and to protect American national security. There were still strong isolationist groups in America, though, who thought that the USA was being needlessly dragged into war. In some cases their opposition was due to their support for Fascism, or a belief that the Fascist threat was being exaggerated, as well as the old desire to keep out of the war. The America First Committee, for example, which was set up in 1940, argued that Britain was fighting to defend not democracy but only its empire. A Nazi victory might be distasteful, but would not actually threaten American security.

There was much discussion about whether the USA should stay neutral. The cartoon in Source 2 presents one point of view.

Nonetheless, American opinion gradually came round to support Roosevelt. The 1939 *Cash and Carry Act* allowed the sale of weapons if the country buying them could pay cash and transport the weapons from the USA. This was intended to help Britain as it had a big enough fleet to transport such supplies. In 1940 Roosevelt gave 50 old destroyers to Britain in exchange for some British military bases, and in March 1941 he put forward his bold Lend-Lease proposal. This allowed America to lend or lease military equipment to Britain without payment until the war was over, since Britain had no money to pay for the goods. Later much the same arrangement was made with Russia.

However, though Americans mostly shared Roosevelt's decision to support Britain and Russia, they were not willing to *fight* with them against Germany and Italy.

Source 2

A cartoon from the *Washington Post*, February 1941, suggests what might happen to the world (and the United States) if America stays out of the war. (The word 'appeasolationists' is made up from putting the words 'appeasers' and 'isolationists' together.)

■ Does the cartoonist think that the USA should enter the war? How can you tell?

Problems in Asia: Japanese expansion

In July 1941, Japan seized French Indochina in South East Asia. American fears of Japanese expansion were now reinforced. America's supplies of tin and rubber from the Far East could be cut off if the Japanese expanded any further. In August 1941, therefore, America banned the sale of oil to Japan. This was a serious blow to Japan's plans for expansion in South East Asia since 80 per cent of its oil came from the United States. The Japanese decided that war with the USA would come sooner or later, and they made up their minds that it should be sooner – and without warning.

Attack on Pearl Harbor

The Japanese fleet launched its surprise attack on the US Pacific fleet at Pearl Harbor on 7 December 1941. Pearl Harbor was an inlet on an island in the Pacific which served as an American naval base. After the attack, the US Congress voted immediately and almost unanimously in favour of war. The very next day, war was declared.

The United States went to war with Japan, but not Germany or Italy. On 11 December, however, the Germans and Italians declared war on America. The separate wars in Asia and Europe had become linked in a global war. The US had become fully involved in what was to prove the most 'popular' war in its history.

American foreign policy after the war

There was general agreement after the war that America could never again afford to turn its back on the affairs of Europe and the rest of the world. Isolationism was now cast aside and America set about carving out a very influential role for itself in world affairs.

The decision to base the new international peace-keeping body, the United Nations, in New York clearly shows this commitment. After the First World War, the United States had refused to join the League of Nations – let alone have its headquarters in its country. Now the USA was to play a role in the United Nations.

Questions

1 Why did many Americans come to accept that Britain should be given some help in the war against Germany?

2 Why could it be argued that America only became involved in international conflicts when its economic interests were threatened?

3 Do you think the United States would have entered the war even if the Japanese had not attacked Pearl Harbor? Explain your answer.

3.2 The American economy at war

Source 1

Poster from Texaco, 1943. It was posted in their factories.

Go ahead, please- TAKE DAY OFF!

1 What is the nationality of the soldier in the poster?

2 How is this confirmed by the style and wording of the caption on the poster?

Source 2

Government poster, 1942. It was designed by Norman Rockwell, America's leading poster artist of the time.

Let's give him Enough and On Time

Roosevelt's New Deal had got Americans used to the idea of a government with greater powers. The Federal Government had created a more centralised administration during the New Deal and was now better placed to extend this role during the war.

The wartime economy was at last able to put an end to the Depression – something which the New Deal had been unable to do. Unemployment in 1939 stood at 9.5 million (17 per cent of the working population). It only began to fall further because the government vastly increased spending on the armed forces during 1940 and 1941. In 1944, unemployment fell to just 670,000. Every American who wanted a job could have one.

Big business and the war effort

During the war, the American economy started to turn out large quantities of military equipment. In 1942 the War Production Board was set up to direct the conversion from peacetime industry to war production. For example, car-makers started to produce tanks. Makers of refrigerators and stoves now produced munitions. In 1939 the tiny air force had just 300 planes. In 1944 the USA built 96,000 aircraft in one year alone – 28,000 more than Germany and Japan put together. Traditional industries such as coal, iron, steel, oil and ship building expanded enormously to deal with the extra $175 billion of government war contracts.

Big business won the vast majority of these contracts, and the influence and profits of America's big corporations increased as a result of the war. Also increased was the faith of Americans in this greater role of government. It seemed that a strong Federal Government, spending lots of the nation's money, was essential to create full employment and a higher standard of living. There was a general agreement that such a role should continue after the war.

Big business and wartime propaganda

During the Second World War huge efforts were made to increase production. Propaganda played an important role. A notable feature of the wartime propaganda was the support given by big business. Companies such as Texaco, Goodyear and, of course, weapons' companies, all had poster campaigns to support the war effort and promote their products (Source 1). Other posters were issued by the government to boost production (Source 2).

The weapons company, Winchester, played a significant and profitable part in the war effort. Source 3 is one of their press advertisements. The text of the advertisement reminds Americans of the importance of Winchester guns in America's previous wars.

Source 3

Advertisement for Winchester weapons, 1943.

Questions

1 a To whom is each poster (Sources 1–3) meant to appeal?
   b Explain the purpose behind each of the posters.

2 What theme do Sources 1 and 2 have in common?

3 In what way is Source 3 different from Sources 1 and 2?

4 Why do you think companies were so keen to produce posters and advertisements of this type (Sources 1–3)?

5 Which of these posters (Sources 1–3) is the most effective in encouraging production for the war effort? Why?

6 Why do you think American businesses and the government put so much emphasis on economic production during the war?

3.3 Black Americans at war

The war provided black Americans with a good opportunity to press their case for civil rights. During the First World War black leaders agreed to suspend their campaign for civil rights, expecting that improvements would come after the war. They did not repeat this mistake. The Congress of Racial Equality (CORE) was set up in 1942 to use non-violent protest to achieve black civil rights, and it started to organise sit-ins against segregated restaurants and theatres.

In 1941, A. Philip Randolph planned a 100,000-strong protest in Washington against the exclusion of black people from jobs in the defence industry. The government was alarmed at the prospect of a mass march, and decided to strike a bargain. Roosevelt agreed to ban discrimination against black people in industrial and government jobs, and to set up a Fair Employment Practice Committee (FEPC) to report on discrimination against black workers in private defence companies. Randolph called off the march.

The FEPC soon discovered that there was widespread discrimination in industry. For example, the Douglas aircraft company employed just 10 black workers in a workforce of 33,000. Not one of Boeing's 41,000 employees was black. The FEPC could not force such companies to employ black people, but it could threaten not to give government contracts to them. This threat led to some improvement.

However, Roosevelt's order on discrimination did not apply to the armed forces. At the start of the war, the army refused to train black officers; the air force would not let them train as pilots; and the navy would only use black servicemen in the kitchens. Black people's blood could not be used for wounded white servicemen. None of the forces would accept black women.

Some of these barriers were broken down by government pressure during the war: 600 black pilots saw combat before the end of the war, and all three of the services eventually had black officers, including women. However, all black servicemen had to fight in segregated, blacks-only units. Though blacks were allowed to die for 'their' country, they were not fit, it seemed, to do so alongside whites. Black Americans would have to wait for the Korean War in 1950 for that 'privilege'!

How did black people react to the Second World War?

Black people had good reason to be angry about their treatment during the early stages of the war. They were discriminated against and barred from certain combat roles in the armed forces. Some blacks, not surprisingly, decided that this war had nothing to do with them, and was not likely to lead to any benefits for them.

The following sources look at the position of black Americans in society, at their attitudes, and at attitudes towards them in the war years. Segregation – separate facilities for blacks and whites – was still prominent during the Second World War, as Source 1 shows:

Source 1

This photograph of a general store was taken in Florida, 1945.

■ How can you tell that this store is meant for black people only?

At first the US Air Force would not accept black pilots. Later in the war the air force finally allowed blacks to serve as pilots – though they were not permitted to fly in the same flight groups as whites.

Source 2

Black pilots taking time out between missions in Italy, 1944.

Source 3 gives the view of a black soldier joining the war:

Source 3

This 'prayer' appeared in a black newspaper in January 1943. It is quoted in H. Zinn, *A People's History of the USA*, 1980.

Draftee's* Prayer

Dear Lord, today
I go to war:
To fight, to die,
Tell me what for?

Dear Lord, I'll fight,
I do not fear
Germans or Japs;
My fears are here.
America!

draftee Someone called up to fight in the war.

Source 4 tells about the response of some black people to America's involvement in the fighting. Racial awareness was clearly a much stronger sentiment than patriotism.

Source 4

Quoted in H. Zinn, *A People's History of the USA*, 1980.

jim-crows 'Jim Crow' laws were the laws in force in the South which discriminated against black people (see also page 21).

disenfranchised Stopped from voting.

A [black] student at a Negro college told his teacher: 'The Army jim-crows* us. The Navy lets us serve only as messmen [kitchen staff]. The Red Cross refuses our blood. Employers and labour unions shut us out. Lynchings continue. We are disenfranchised,** jim-crowed, spat upon. What more could Hitler do than that?'

NAACP [National Association for the Advancement of Colored People] leader Walter White repeated this to a black audience of several thousand people in the Midwest, thinking they would disapprove, but instead, as he recalled: 'To my surprise and dismay the audience burst into such applause that it took me some thirty or forty seconds to quiet it.'

Questions

1 What does Source 2 suggest about changes in attitude towards black people since the beginning of the war?

2 Does Source 1 support or contradict your answer to Question 1? Explain your answer.

3 Explain what the writer of the 'prayer' in Source 3 might have meant by the last two lines.

4 What do you suppose the black student in Source 4 meant by 'What more could Hitler do than that?'?

5 How might the black student quoted in Source 4 have reacted to (i) Source 2; (ii) Source 3? Explain your answer.

6 What do Sources 1–4 suggest about changes in (i) attitudes *to* black people; (ii) attitudes *of* black people? Explain your answer.

3.4 Women at war

The role of women in American society before the war was a conventional one. Women were mainly concerned with the home in their role as wives and mothers. Few women followed careers. Job opportunities were usually in the typically 'female' or caring professions such as teaching and nursing, or in clerical and secretarial work.

The call for many hands

As millions of men joined the armed forces in 1941, more workers were needed to fill their places in industry. Women were called on to satisfy this urgent demand for labour. This in turn challenged 'traditional' views of women.

Between 1910 and 1940, the proportion of women in the workforce had barely altered. This all changed in 1941. The war opened up many new areas of employment for working class women, especially in producing munitions. (Middle class women found war work in industry less attractive.) The pay in munitions factories was much higher than that normally paid to women for typically 'female' occupations such as secretarial and domestic work.

Source 1

Women perform mass inspection of propellors, 1942.

Old barriers broke down rapidly as women became machinists, lumberjacks and railway track workers – entering these and other occupations previously reserved for men. By 1942, a poll showed that 60 per cent of Americans (men and women) were in favour of hiring married women in war industries. This reflected a considerable change in attitudes.

Between 1940 and 1945 the number of women in the workforce increased from 12 million to 18.5 million, and women made up a third of the nation's labour force. Most of their jobs were in shipyards, aircraft factories and armaments depots. In the shipyards, for example, women performed every conceivable job, from welding and assembling to operating cranes and running the offices. In 1939, only 36 women were employed in ship construction. By the end of 1942, this number had increased to nearly 200,000.

Because machinery was now automated, brute strength was no longer needed to operate it and women were able to do the work – much of it skilled – without difficulty.

Women also found their way into the armed forces in large numbers. Some 300,000 served in the women's sections of the army, navy and the nursing corps, and 25 per cent of these served overseas. Black women were allowed to serve as nurses after 1941, but only to nurse black soldiers.

Conditions for some working women were improved during the war. Four US states made equal pay for women compulsory, and others protected women from discrimination in jobs.

Returning to the home

Despite these developments during the war, most women seemed to think it was their duty to give up their jobs after the war, to provide work for their returning men.

A 1946 opinion poll found the following attitudes among men and women. Each person interviewed was asked, 'On the whole, who do you think has the most interesting time: the woman who is holding a full-time job, or the woman who is running a home?'

Source 2

J. P. Diggins, *The Proud Decades*, 1989.

■ These statistics provide a snapshot of opinion in 1946. Why are they less useful, though, as evidence of *changing attitudes*?

Who has a more interesting time?

People questioned	Women with full-time job	Women running a home	No difference	Don't know
Men	27%	49%	8%	15%
Women	32%	50%	8%	10.5%

The numbers in industry declined once the war was over, but the percentage of women in the labour force in 1950 was still some 2 per cent higher than it had been in 1940 – at 29 per cent. The percentage of married women who had jobs outside the home continued to increase after the war:

Source 3

Percentage of married women who had jobs outside the home.

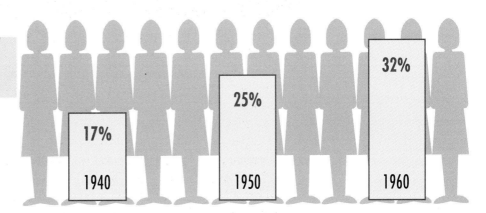

Even if many women did seem content to go back to their traditional role as home-maker, the confidence which came with the responsible and skilled work they did during the war stayed with them.

To what extent did the role of women change as a result of the war?

There is no doubt that the role of women changed during the Second World War, as many women took on crucial work for the war effort. But just how far did their role change? And was it a lasting change? Sources 4–8 look at the role of women before, during and after the war.

Look first at Source 4. It is from a tape-recording made by Studs Terkel, an oral historian who interviews ordinary Americans about their past lives. In it, a woman who worked in a munitions factory during the war describes her experiences.

Source 4

Peggy Terry describes her work in a munitions factory in Kentucky during the war. Quoted in Studs Terkel, *The Good War*, 1985.

I pulled a lot of gadgets on a machine. The shell slid under and powder went into it. Another lever you pulled stamped it down. Then it moved on a conveyor belt to another building where the detonator was dropped in. You did this over and over.

Tetryl was one of the ingredients and it turned us orange …. Our hair was orange. Our hands, our face, our neck just turned orange, even our eyeballs. We never questioned …. The only thing we worried about was other women thinking we had dyed our hair. Back then it was a disgrace if you dyed your hair ….

I remember a woman saying on the bus that she hoped the war didn't end until she got her refrigerator paid for.

Now look at Sources 5 and 6. Source 5 is an advertisement for *Irresistible* perfume. The image of women which it popularises is typical of many advertisements which appeared in the late 1930s, before America went to war.

Source 5

Perfume advertisement, 1937.

■ Compare Source 5 with the image projected by Source 6, an advertisement which appeared two years after America entered the war.

Source 6

An advertisment for silver plate cutlery, 1943.

Many popular magazines in the 1930s put pictures of women on their covers in an attempt to boost sales. These 'cover girls' were invariably young and good-looking. Sources 7 and 8 show two ways in which cover girls were used during the war. Source 7 shows 'Rosie the Riveter', a fictional character who featured in government documentaries to encourage reluctant women to do war industry work. Here she appears on the cover of a leading magazine:

Source 7

Cover from the *Sunday Evening Post*, 1943. Rosie was painted by Norman Rockwell.

Women, as you can see from Source 8, were admitted into the various armed services. These army and navy recruits were photographed in 1944, during a competition to choose that year's 'Service Cover Girl'.

Source 8

Competitors in the 'Service Cover Girl' contest of 1944. The contest was held to find the most attractive woman in the US armed services. It was won, the original caption tells us, by Corporal Lisa Rutherford.

Questions

1 What image of women in 1937 does Source 5 give?

2 What does Source 6 suggest about the way the war affected women?

3 How do the images of women in Sources 6 and 7 differ?

4 In what ways does Source 8 both support and disagree with Source 6 about the role of women during the war?

5 Which sources most support Source 4 about the role of women during the war? Explain your answer.

6 'These sources tell us little about how the war affected the lives of American women.' What is your view of this statement? Give reasons for your answer.

3.5 The legacy of the Second World War

Before the war the United States each year spent less than 1 per cent of its GNP on military expenditure. Understandably, during the war this proportion increased to 30 per cent of GNP. What is more surprising is that military expenditure remained much higher after the war than it had been before it. In the 40 years after 1945, the United States spent between 8 and 20 per cent of its GNP on the military, and so maintained the largest ever peacetime armed forces.

Another result of the war was that black people were encouraged to press much harder for their rights. The creation of the Fair Employment Practice Committee (FEPC) in 1941 established the notion that the Federal Government should involve itself in civil rights issues. Some white Americans also came to realise that if the war had been fought to defend freedom and democracy against Nazi tyranny, then black people deserved a greater share of that freedom if the war was to have any real meaning.

In political terms, the most important result of the war was that Americans came to accept the idea of 'big government'. Roosevelt, who died a few weeks before the surrender of Germany in April 1945, had given Americans faith in the Federal Government, after the despair of the Depression. The people believed that the Federal Government could and should solve economic and social problems.

The rationing of essential items such as meat, petrol and tyres was accepted by Americans as being both fair and patriotic. The idea that money could no longer buy you everything was a new one for Americans – though, as in Britain, the black market soon sprang up to provide rationed goods at much higher prices for those who could afford them. Nonetheless, this new role for government was a tradition which both President Truman and President Kennedy were to carry on.

Questions

1 How did attitudes to the role of the government change during the war?

2 Why could black people accuse the US Government of having double standards in its treatment of them during the war?

3 Can you suggest any reason why US military spending remained so high in the decades after the Second World War?

4 Can you give any examples of what the author means by 'big government'?

3.6 Review activity

What changes took place in the United States during the war? How important were they?

	Situation before the war	Did the war lead to an important change?	Evidence for or against
1 Role of the Federal Government	Before Roosevelt, most Americans thought that governments should not 'interfere' in the economy or try to make society fairer for disadvantaged groups like black people and the poor. This was beginning to change by the outbreak of the war.		
2 Isolationism			
3 Position of women			
4 Position of black people			

1 Copy the chart above.

2 Fill in the blank columns to answer the questions, using the information in this unit. (One of the boxes has been filled in already.)

Unit 4 · 'Reds' and 'blacks'

The social tensions of the 1920s and 1930s did not all disappear with the Second World War. The late 1940s and early 1950s saw a revival of the 'Red Scare' of the 1920s. Another issue of the 1920s – race – also returned to dominate American politics in the 1950s.

The 'Red Scare' of the 1920s was brought about mainly by events *inside* the United States (see page 20). The anti-Communist hysteria of the 1950s, on the other hand, was sparked off by events *outside* the United States, such as the Berlin Blockade in 1948 and the Communist victory in China in 1949. These events led to real fears of nuclear war with Communist Russia.

Source 1

Rising fears: the USA tested their first atomic bomb on Bikini in the Pacific, 1946. In 1949, the Soviet Union tested their first atomic bomb. The USA – alarmed – responded by developing the more deadly hydrogen bomb, or H bomb, which was first tested in 1952. As Cold War tensions rose, so did the superpowers' spending on nuclear weapons.

In the almost hysterical climate of the 1950s it was even harder to press for black people's rights, and some white conservatives accused the Civil Rights Movement of being Communist-led. Presidents such as Truman and Kennedy had great plans to help the poor and disadvantaged. But they were up against a Congress determined to undermine their reform programmes. Presidents were so powerless against Congress that they sometimes seemed little more than 'prisoners' in the White House.

4.1 Prisoners in the White House? – the post-war presidents

President Truman and the 'Fair Deal'

Harry Truman, elected as Vice-President in 1944, became President on the death of Roosevelt in April 1945. Like Roosevelt, he was a Democrat. Little was known about Truman, and people doubted his ability to cope with such an important office. However, he was to prove his critics wrong during the next seven years. The new president was a strong supporter of the New Deal, and he shared Roosevelt's belief that the Federal Government had a responsibility to help the poor, control the power of big business, and bring about a fairer society. Indeed, Truman described his policy as 'the Fair Deal'.

Truman's biggest problem in bringing about the 'Fair Deal' was the opposition of Congress (the House of Representatives and the Senate together). In 1946, for the first time in sixteen years, Congress had a majority of Republican members. They rejected Truman's plans to spend $2,700 million to improve the living conditions and health of the poor. He could achieve few of his policies as long as Congress was hostile to him.

Under the American political system, it has always been possible for the party supporting the President to be outnumbered in Congress by the Opposition. This is because the President and the Congress are elected at different times and in different circumstances. (See page 47.)

1948: a surprise victory for the Democrats

Truman's first three years as President had not been a startling success as far as domestic politics were concerned. Truman was not therefore expected to win the presidential election of 1948 – especially since there were two rival candidates for Democratic votes. Surprisingly, though, Truman did win, beating the Republican candidate, Thomas Dewey, by 2 million votes. Truman's strong leadership of the United States in the emerging Cold War against Communist Russia, and the fact that many black people and union members were behind him, swung support in his favour.

Source 2

Truman won the 1948 election, but the *Chicago Daily Tribune* went to press on the night of the election convinced that his opponent Dewey would win. A delighted Truman, pictured here the following morning, was able to prove the newspaper wrong.

■ Why do you think that the *Chicago Daily Tribune* (and many others) were convinced that Truman would lose the election?

There was more good news for Truman when his Democratic Party won a majority of seats in Congress. At last some of his 'Fair Deal' programme could be approved. The minimum wage was raised from 40 cents an hour to 75 cents, social security benefits were increased, and money was allocated to clear slums and build low-rent housing.

However, Congress did not approve all of the President's policies. His proposal to set up a national health insurance scheme was defeated, and his attempt to guarantee greater civil rights for blacks was turned down by Congress because Southern Democrats voted against it. Even though these Democrats belonged to the same party as Truman, the fact that they came from the South made them unwilling to support civil rights policies. This added considerably to the problems faced by Democrat presidents keen to help black people. There was one success in the area of civil rights, though. The army was finally desegregated. Black soldiers could now serve (and die) alongside white soldiers in the same units.

President Eisenhower: the 'genial general'

The popular American general and war hero, Dwight Eisenhower, who led the Allied Forces to victory in the Second World War, was chosen by the Republicans to stand as their candidate for the 1952 presidential election. Eisenhower's war record was a good vote-winner: few people had a clear idea of what he actually stood for (Source 3). He was popular, though. All across America, car stickers simply announced, 'I like Ike' (Eisenhower).

Eisenhower was a moderate Republican who wanted to create a balance between the needs of private business and the role of the government. This meant that he would allow the government to get involved in social and economic issues if necessary, but preferred to allow businesses to run their own affairs without government interference.

1952: landslide for the Republicans

Eisenhower won the 1952 presidential election with a massive majority of nearly 7 million votes, ending twenty years of Democrat rule.

He may have been popular, but the press was unsure what Eisenhower's real political views were, as Source 3 illustrates. The Republican campaign managers, too, seem to have had trouble thinking up ideas for the 1952 election, as Source 4 shows:

Source 3

Cartoon in *News Chronicle*, 1952. This British cartoon by the socialist cartoonist, Vicky, makes fun of the uncertainty over which political party – Republican or Democrat – Eisenhower would join once he retired from the army and stood for President.

Source 4

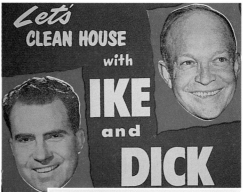

Campaign poster for the 1952 presidential election. This poster shows Dwight Eisenhower ('Ike', top right) and Richard Nixon ('Dick'), his vice-presidential candidate, promising to 'clean house'.

■ How does Vicky show the uncertainty about Eisenhower's political intentions?

■ Do you think this poster would have played a big part in Eisenhower's overwhelming election victory? Explain your answer.

Eisenhower and 'modern Republicanism'

Eisenhower's approach was a mixture of 'conservative' and 'liberal' measures. He cut taxes on businesses and wealthy individuals, and ended controls on wages and prices, as businesses were 'set free' from government controls. These 'conservative' policies were balanced by more 'liberal' ones. Social security benefits were increased and extended to include another 10 million people, and the minimum wage was increased from 75 cents an hour to $1.00.

Eisenhower also proposed spending federal money on school buildings but the Democrats, who controlled Congress from 1954, opposed the bill. They objected because the schools were still racially segregated and not entitled, therefore, to government money. Some Republicans also opposed the bill because they objected to government money being spent in an area (education) which was under the control of the states.

Questions

1 Why could black people claim that the way they were treated under Truman and Eisenhower was 'unconstitutional' (against the Constitution)?

2 Why would Southern Democrats in Congress have voted against Truman's bill to give greater rights to black people?

3 Why was proposing civil rights legislation always likely to be a problem for Democrat presidents?

4 Why could Eisenhower's policies of 'modern Republicanism' be described as a blend of 'rugged individualism' and Roosevelt's 'big government' approach?

5 To what extent were the presidents of this period – Truman and Eisenhower – 'prisoners in the White House'? Why?

4.2 Cold War and the Communist 'menace'

From World War to Cold War

Two countries emerged from the Second World War as 'superpowers': the United States and the Soviet Union. America in particular was far stronger in wealth, resources and manpower than any of the countries in Europe. The political differences between the USA and the Soviet Union after the war were to mark a new 'war' that was to last for many years – the 'Cold War'.

The Cold War was so called because it was a period of great tension, or hostility, but it involved no actual fighting. Both superpowers were suspicious and fearful of each other. America feared that the Soviet Union would encourage Communists worldwide to take over power – either by taking control of governments in their own countries, or through war. The Soviet Union, on the other hand, feared that America would try to crush Communism abroad. The USA was particularly anxious when the Soviet Union spread its control into Eastern Europe in the 1940s and 1950s. The Soviet Union, feeling under threat itself, wanted Eastern Europe as a buffer against the West.

Free speech under threat

When President Truman took office, the Cold War was just beginning. He took a firm stand against efforts by the Soviet Union to spread Communist influence in Europe and this clearly went down well with American voters. Truman also introduced the *Federal Employee Loyalty Program* in 1947. This was designed to identify and dismiss any 'security risks' (Communists) working for the Federal Government. Every person taking on a new job in the civil service or government would also be investigated.

The Senate's House Un-American Activities Committee (HUAC) had been investigating Communist 'infiltration' of Hollywood since 1947. This led to many actors 'confessing' their sympathies for, or membership of, the Communist Party. Others, like the actor and future president Ronald Reagan, were quick to tell HUAC of suspected Communists in the film industry. Other non-Communist actors, such as Humphrey Bogart and Lauren Bacall, bravely protested against this 'un-American' attack on people's right to believe what they wanted.

Source 1

This photograph, taken in October 1947, shows leading Hollywood actors and actresses protesting against the HUAC investigation into alleged Communism in the film industry. Humphrey Bogart and Lauren Bacall (front centre) were very popular stars at this time.

■ Why could their action be considered courageous?

Why was fear of Communism so strong?

Why were Americans' reactions to Communism so strong? 'Better dead than Red' was a common saying in the United States in the late 1940s and the 1950s. Many Americans were *so* opposed to Communism that they would rather be dead than live under Communist rule. Why?

Traitors and spies?

American concerns about Communism were increased during 1948 when the Russians 'blockaded' West Berlin in Germany. The Russians tried to drive the Western powers out of Berlin so that they could fully take over. Open war almost broke out between the two superpowers.

In 1948, Alger Hiss, a former official of the US State Department (responsible for Foreign Affairs), was accused by a former Communist of handing over more that 200 secret State Department documents to him and of being a Communist. Hiss denied both charges. He was sentenced to five years in prison for perjury (lying under oath) but was never convicted of being a spy for Russia. In 1992, Russian military intelligence documents were made public, suggesting that Hiss had no link with Russia's spy network after all.

Two events in 1949 greatly increased American fears about the Communist 'threat'. Firstly, Chinese Communists took power in China. Secondly, the Russians exploded their first test atomic bomb – up until then only the USA had possessed this terrible weapon. The situation turned even more threatening when in 1950 Communist North Korea invaded pro-American South Korea.

Concern about Communists in high places reached a peak in 1950 when an American husband and wife, Julius and Ethel Rosenberg, were convicted of selling nuclear weapon secrets to the Soviet Union (then an *ally* of the USA) during the Second World War. They were both executed by the electric chair in 1953.

All that was needed now was for someone to come along and exploit these fears of Communism to make a political career for himself.

The McCarthy 'witch-hunts'

In 1950, an ambitious and dishonest Republican Senator, Joseph McCarthy, claimed he had a list of 205 members of the Communist Party of the United States who worked for the State Department. McCarthy never produced any evidence for this claim but he knew that the American public was ready to believe him in the climate of the time. His fellow Republicans in Congress were also ready to back him. The Democrats had been in power for seventeen years, and the Republicans were desperate to use anything they could against Truman's government.

Those people named by McCarthy had their lives ruined. In all, 2,375 men and women were summoned to appear before the Senate's House Un-American Activities Committee (HUAC). This was enough to cost them their jobs. Some 400 Americans were sentenced to terms in jail. The chance of a fair trial was remote – lawyers were afraid that to defend an individual accused of being a Communist would ruin their careers, too.

The press, like the public, was hostile to Communists. Source 2 expresses some widespread fears of the time.

McCarthy soon turned public opinion against himself. Televised hearings of his Senate Investigating Committee showed him to be a bully and a liar. The last straw came when he claimed that the army had been infiltrated by Communists, and that the Republican President at the

Source 2

American cartoon, 1950s, shows a Communist swearing an oath of loyalty to the United States. The hammer and sickle symbol on his back also appeared on the Soviet flag.

■ Why are we meant to assume that the man is not really loyal to the United States?

time, Eisenhower, knew about it and did nothing. McCarthy's behaviour was condemned by the Senate in 1954 and he was forced out of public life.

By then, though, the damage had been done. Some 9,500 civil servants had been dismissed and another 15,000 had resigned; 600 teachers had lost their jobs and many fine actors and scriptwriters were unable to work in the film industry again. Charlie Chaplin, the British comedian, came under suspicion too. Angered, he left the United States, never to work there again.

Source 3

Cartoon from the Russian magazine *Krokodil*, 1951. Policemen stare out through the eyes of the Statue of Liberty – a striking comment on the effects of McCarthy's anti-Communist campaign.

1 Why do you think the cartoonist chose to show the Statue of Liberty? What is its significance?

2 What general point do you think the cartoonist was making?

КРОКОДИЛ

The influence of McCarthyism

McCarthy's influence did not disappear with him. The 1950 *McCarran Internal Security Act* – forcing organisations regarded as fronts for Communism to register with the government and provide a list of members – remained effective, as did the 1954 *Communist Control Act*, which banned the Communist Party altogether.

McCarthy's appeal had much to do with Americans' traditional distrust of the kind of middle class intellectuals (professional people such as writers, teachers, lawyers and journalists) who supported left-wing causes. McCarthy described them as 'twisted-thinking eggheads' who were 'born with silver spoons in their mouths'.

McCarthy's impact was a particularly harmful one for the United States since it made the persecution of people for their beliefs seem justifiable, and it undermined the spirit of tolerance which had made the United States a proud nation. American politicians would continue to be frightened of being called a 'Commie' or being 'soft on Communism' for merely stating their sympathy for the poor, blacks or trade unionists.

It did not take long for some Conservatives, especially in the South, to claim that support for the rights of black Americans was also 'un-American'. In some states, black civil rights' organisations were treated as though they were Communist ones, and anti-Communist laws were used against them.

Questions

1 Why were Americans more likely to support anti-Communism in the early 1950s than in 1945?

2 Why could it be argued that the House Un-American Activities Committee which investigated suspected Communists was itself 'un-American'?

4.3 Black Americans in the 1950s

You have read about the horrific racism that disfigured American society in the 1920s (Unit 1.4). You have followed the impact on black Americans of the Depression (Unit 2.3) and the Second World War (Unit 3.3). How far had their lives changed by the 1950s?

Did life improve for black people between the 1920s and the 1950s?

The race riot described below was one of 25 which took place right across the country in 1919. These riots between black people and white people were the worst that had taken place up to that time.

Segregation and inferior facilities for black people were a fact of life in

Source 1

Extract written by a black historian, John Hope Franklin, in *From Slavery to Freedom: A History of Negro Americans*, 1980.

In Omaha a [white] mob almost completely destroyed the county courthouse by fire in order to secure [seize] a Negro who was in jail on the charge of attacking a white girl. The group succeeded in seizing him, whereupon he was dragged through the streets, shot more than a thousand times, and mutilated beyond recognition. He was finally hanged downtown at one of the busiest intersections [crossroads].

the South, as Sources 2 and 3 show. First, Martin Luther King, the great civil rights leader, describes life for a typical black person growing up in the Southern city of Birmingham, Alabama, after the Second World War.

Source 2

Martin Luther King, speaking in 1963.

You would be born into a jim-crow hospital to parents who probably lived in a ghetto. You would attend a jim-crow school .... You would spend your childhood playing mainly in the streets because the 'colored' parks were absolutely inadequate ....

If you wanted a job in this city – one of the greatest iron- and steel-producing centres in the nation – you had better settle on doing menial work as a porter or labourer. If you were fortunate enough to get a job you could expect that promotion ... would come, not to you, but to a white employee regardless of your comparative talents. On your job, you would eat in a separate place and use a water fountain and lavatory labelled 'Colored' ....

You would be confronted with every conceivable obstacle to taking that most important walk a Negro American can take today – the walk to the ballot box ....

Coretta Scott King was the wife of Martin Luther King. She wrote this account of her segregated education in the South in the 1930s:

Source 3

From C. Scott King, *My Life with Martin Luther King*, 1969.

■ How does Coretta King suggest that segregation had a good as well as a bad side for black people?

We were in some respects luckier than many of the supposedly integrated children in the ghetto schools up north. In many instances, at least what we were taught was planned for us by our own people, *by* blacks *for* blacks. Many of our schools even had courses in black history.

The [black] children of the northern slums were educated under a mass-produced system designed for the majority of white students, which was totally irrelevant to their experiences and which they could neither identify with nor adapt to; and nobody cared whether they did or did not.

Source 4 describes the life of a black family of sixteen, living in a three-room shack in Mississippi in the early 1940s. They survived on a basic income of just $230 a year – at a time when the average car worker's annual wage was $1,690.

Source 4

Newspaper report, quoted in J. C. Furnas, *How America Lives*, 1943.

There were no blankets all winter, but sacks helped a little ... with the wind whistling through the wide cracks in the floor. Further protection against the wind is given by newspapers plastered all over the walls with flour paste .... Lack of shoes usually keeps them from school in winter, and only the children over 14 know much about reading and writing; their parents nothing at all.

Source 5

This drinking fountain was for black people only. It is a typical example of segregated life in the South.

The 'Jim Crow' laws – which dated back to the 1890s – were still in practice in many parts of the South after the Second World War, as Source 5 shows. As in the 1920s, racial violence also continued after the war. This, and the difficulty of halting discrimination and violence, is reflected in Source 6.

Source 6

Cartoon from the *Milwaukee Journal*, 1948.

'The Civil Rights Bill Would Destroy Our Southern Way of Life, Suh!'

In Mississippi in 1955, a 14-year-old black boy, Emmett Till from Chicago, was beaten to death for whistling at a white woman. A black girl who was 14 herself at the time remembers her reaction to the murder:

Source 7

Anne Moody, *Coming of Age in Mississippi*, 1968.

1 What was Anne Moody's greatest fear? What does this suggest about the position of black people in the 1950s?

2 What was her attitude to those black people who did not stand up for their rights?

Before Emmett Till's murder, I had known the fear of hunger, hell, and the Devil. But now there was a new fear known to me – the fear of being killed just because I was black. This was the worst of my fears …. I hated the white men who had killed Emmett Till …. But I also hated Negroes. I hated them for not standing up and not doing something about the murders … it was at this stage in my life that I began to look upon Negro men as cowards. I could not respect them for smiling in a white man's face, addressing them as Mr So-and-So, saying yessuh and nossuh ….

The next extract is by a socialist, Michael Harrington. He investigated poverty in the USA in 1962. He set out deliberately, he wrote, to find the American poor and describe the injustice of their lives.

Source 8

From M. Harrington, *The Other America*, 1962.

The Negro is poor because he is black; that is obvious enough …. The laws against colour can be removed, but that will still leave the poverty which has long been the consequence of colour. As long as this is the case, being born a Negro will continue to be the greatest disadvantage that the United States imposes on a man.

Source 9 shows the number of people, black and white, living below the 'poverty line' in 1959.

Source 9

Statistics from US Department of Commerce; reproduced in *Statistical Abstract of the United States*, 1970.

Living below the poverty line, 1959

Racial group	Number of people living below the poverty line (in millions)	Percentage of people living below the poverty line (%)
White	28.5	18
Black and other races	11	56

Questions

1 What does Source 2 tell you about the treatment and position of black people in the 1950s?

2 What do Sources 3 and 7 tell you about growing up as a black person in the United States earlier in this century?

3 Harrington writes, 'The Negro is poor because he is black; that is obvious' (Source 8). What was the link between being black and being poor?

4 Which source best supports the point made by the writer in Source 8? Explain your answer.

5 What do Sources 1–9 tell you about changes (if any) in the situation of black people between the 1920s and the 1950s?

4.4 The Civil Rights Movement

The year 1954 was a momentous one in the history of black Americans. In that year the Supreme Court finally declared that the existence of separate (or 'segregated') schools for white and black children was against the Constitution, and therefore illegal. It was the first victory in a campaign for black people's rights known as the Civil Rights Movement.

A legal victory for black people

The Supreme Court's decision came about as the result of a test case: *Brown versus the Board of Education of Topeka* in 1954. The case involved Oliver Brown of Topeka, Kansas, who sued the city school board for forbidding his 8-year-old daughter, who was black, from attending a nearby white school. Instead the daughter had been forced to attend a school much further away.

This important case was brought to the Supreme Court by an organisation called the National Association for the Advancement of Colored People (NAACP). A black lawyer, Thurgood Marshall, presented the case against school segregation, and won. The Supreme Court decided that segregated education deprived children of 'the equal protection of the laws guaranteed by the Fourteenth Amendment' of the American Constitution. The following year, the Court ordered *all* states with segregated education to integrate their schools by allowing black and white children to attend the same schools.

This policy was strongly opposed in the Southern States where there were not only segregated schools but segregated bars, fountains, toilets and even whites-only seats on buses. The individual states tried to ignore the Supreme Court ruling, and looked for all kinds of loopholes to avoid desegregating schools. In Virginia, for example, some state schools were changed into private ones to avoid desegregating.

The first real test of President Eisenhower's and the Federal Government's determination to see this new law enforced came in 1957 at Little Rock, Arkansas.

The challenge at Little Rock, 1957

In 1957, nine black pupils had been stopped from joining the all-white Central High School at Little Rock. The Federal Government ordered the state Governor to let the children enrol. He refused, and was well supported by the local white population. So Eisenhower sent in 10,000 National Guardsmen and 1,000 paratroopers to make sure that the nine black teenagers joined the school.

Eisenhower's decision showed how much the power of the Federal Government was increasing at the expense of states' rights. Nonetheless, the success was limited. By 1961 there were still no black children in white schools in the states of Alabama, Mississippi or Carolina; progress towards desegregation after Little Rock was extremely slow. Though there were some 2 million black school children in the South in 1960, a mere 2,600 of these went to integrated schools with whites.

Source 1

Elizabeth Eckford, one of the nine black students who tried to enrol in the all-white school at Little Rock. Here she is directed away from the school by an Arkansas State Guardsman. These soldiers were sent to the school by the Governor of Arkansas. He claimed this was to prevent racial conflict, by stopping black students from enrolling in the school.

■ What is another possible interpretation of the Governor's action?

Source 2

This photograph of the Central High School, Little Rock, was taken three weeks after the photograph above (Source 1). Here, the soldiers shown are not State Guardsmen but *federal* troops sent to make sure that the black students gained entry to the school.

■ What indications are there in this photograph that Eisenhower was *determined* to enforce the Supreme Court ruling on desegregation?

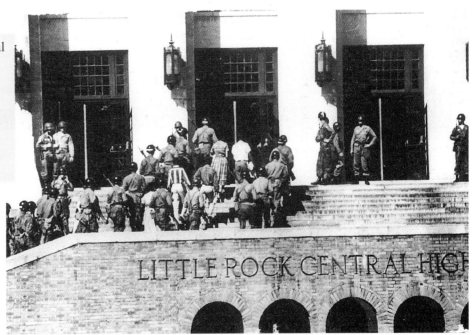

'A friendly face somewhere in the mob'

It is easy for people today to see an incident like Little Rock only for its historical importance, and to forget the courage of the individuals involved. Troops had to be stationed inside the Central High School and they escorted the nine black children everywhere they went for a whole year to protect them from harassment by white students.

The terror of that first day when the nine black students tried to enrol in the school is remembered in Source 3 by 14-year-old Elizabeth Eckford.

Source 3

Elizabeth Eckford, 1957, quoted in Daisy Bates, *The Long Shadow of Little Rock*, 1962.

They glared at me with a mean look and I was very frightened and didn't know what to do. I turned around and the crowd came toward me. They moved closer and closer. Somebody started yelling 'Lynch her! Lynch her!' I tried to see a friendly face somewhere in the mob – someone maybe who would help. I looked into the face of an old woman and it seemed a kind face. But when I looked at her again, she spat at me.

A rising tide

The Supreme Court's ruling against segregation in schools had come about as a result of the test case which was brought by the National Association for the Advancement of Colored People (see page 76). It was a great legal victory for black people.

The NAACP had been founded in 1909. It provided funding and support for many civil rights court cases in the 1950s. At the law school at Howard University in Washington DC, a new generation of determined black lawyers received the training they needed to challenge segregation through the law courts. They scored several successes for black civil rights.

However, the campaign to abolish segregation through the law was inevitably very slow. Even if the black lawyers won, it was difficult to enforce the law. And the campaign involved only a tiny number of well-educated people. Meanwhile, tens of thousands of black Americans were keen to get involved with some form of protest action. They soon had their chance. The first major event of popular protest was the Montgomery Bus Boycott.

The Montgomery Bus Boycott, 1955

In 1955, Rosa Parks, a black woman travelling on a bus in Montgomery, refused to move from her seat to give it to a white man (when the white seats were all taken, black passengers were supposed to give up their seats for white passengers). Parks was arrested.

Angry black women urged their local leaders to act. So a 26-year-old Baptist pastor, Martin Luther King, organised a boycott of the bus company. In this boycott, black people, who provided 75 per cent of the company's business, refused to use buses. They walked or shared cars instead. The rest of America and the world followed the events on television, radio and in the newspapers: life in the Deep South came under the international spotlight. After a year-long boycott the bus company weakened, and the Supreme Court declared that segregated buses, like schools, were against the Constitution.

Black people had won a momentous victory – not by physical violence, but by peaceful mass protest.

In 1957, Eisenhower introduced the first *Civil Rights Act* since 1875. It created a Federal Civil Rights Commission to prosecute those who denied any citizens their rights – especially their right to vote. The Act itself did not achieve much but it did show that the Federal Government was no longer willing to allow the Southern States to do as they pleased as far as race relations were concerned.

Martin Luther King and 'direct action'

The Montgomery Bus Boycott produced a new leader: Martin Luther King. He did not believe in the use of violence. He was a Christian and a pacifist. He realised that legal battles in the courts would be slow – and that the laws were not always enforced, anyway. Physical violence was wrong. The answer was 'direct action' and non-violent protest against racial discrimination.

In 1957, along with other clergy from Southern States, he formed the Southern Christian Leadership Conference (SCLC) to fight against racial segregation. He declared that black people were tired of '300 years of humiliation, abuse and deprivation'. They wanted 'absolute and immediate freedom and equality … right here in this land today ….'

Non-violent protests

Sit-in protests were an effective method of non-violent protest. In 1960, four black students asked to be served at a Woolworths lunch counter in Greensboro, reserved for white customers only. When they were refused service by the black waitress, they staged a sit-in demonstration in the cafeteria. Two days later, 85 black and white students staged another sit-in protest. Within eighteen months, 70,000 had taken part in similar sit-ins against segregated services across the South and 3,000 had been arrested. The mass protests once again drew the attention of the country's media to other injustices endured by black people.

Source 4

Three civil rights supporters sit at a lunch counter reserved for whites at a Woolworths store in Jackson, Mississippi, in May 1963. One white youth is about to pour a can of drink over the head of the woman in the middle. They have already been smeared with sauce and mustard and sprayed with paint. After three hours the crowd began to beat the man.

■ Does the picture suggest why the Civil Rights Movement eventually won the support of so many Americans?

Source 5

Four university professors and three black students being arrested in 1968 for using a whites-only waiting room.

■ What does this photograph tell you about the strengths and weaknesses of the Civil Rights Movement? (Clue: think about the profession of the protestors.)

The violent reaction of white opponents of desegregation led to a great deal of national publicity for the civil rights protesters. Their refusal to use violence impressed many – especially people abroad.

The protesters may have won some victories, but much still remained to be done in other, even more important areas where black people faced discrimination. For example, literacy tests were still commonly used in the South to prevent them from voting, and they still did not have equal opportunities in jobs. In 1960, the unemployment rate for the population was 5.5 per cent. For black people it was 11 per cent.

Why were there different attitudes to the Civil Rights Movement?

Attitudes to the Civil Rights Movement in the USA varied a great deal. For example, black people within the movement disagreed over what strategy to use. Not all Southern whites were opposed to the movement – though clearly a great many were.

The key issue here is to try and understand why there were these different responses. What social, economic, political or religious ideas led to people's different attitudes?

Below, Robert Zellner describes his experiences in the early 1960s. Zellner was white. His grandfather had been a member of the Ku Klux Klan; his father was a Southern Christian preacher. As a university student, Zellner and four other white students became involved in the Civil Rights Movement during 1960–61. They were asked to leave by the university authorities in Alabama.

Source 6

Robert Zellner, interviewed in 1978, quoted in *The Eyes on the Prize* (a collection of speeches, documents and interviews from the Civil Rights Movement), 1991.

So out of the five [white] guys involved .... I was the only person out of the five that graduated. One attempted suicide. The others got tremendous pressure from their families. Mine was the only family that backed me up in the whole thing. In a sense ... they gave no white Southerner of that period any choice. If you backed the system at all you had two choices: you either agreed with the system absolutely and completely, or you became a rebel, a complete outlaw and that's the way I went.

What was the role of violence in the struggle? Should physical force be used to succeed? The following sources give two contrasting views. Robert Williams was a black activist in the Civil Rights Movement. He was one of the few activists who argued against the non-violent tactics of the movement. He thought black people needed to use force. He was suspended from the National Association for the Advancement of Colored People (NAACP). This was his opinion:

Source 7

Robert Williams, in *Liberation* (a magazine), 1959, quoted in *The Eyes on the Prize*, 1991.

I believe Negroes must be willing to defend themselves, their women, their children and their homes. They must be willing to die and to kill in repelling their assailants [attackers]. Negroes *must* protect themselves, it is obvious that the Federal Government will not put an end to lynching; therefore it becomes necessary for us to stop lynching with violence.

Martin Luther King wrote in the same magazine, *Liberation*, giving his view on the role of violence in the struggle for black rights:

Source 8

Martin Luther King, in *Liberation*, 1959, quoted in *The Eyes on the Prize*, 1991.

When the Negro uses force in self-defence he does not lose support – he may even win it, by the courage and self-respect it reflects. When he seeks to start violence he ... inevitably is blamed for its consequences. It is unfortunately true that however the Negro acts, his struggle will not be free of violence begun by his enemies, and he will need great courage and willingness to defeat this violence. But if he seeks it and organises it, he cannot win ....

The *New York Times* ran the report in Source 9. It tells of the reaction of white people outside Little Rock Central High School as the black children entered the school (see also page 77).

Source 9

New York Times, September 1957.

A man yelled: 'Look, they're going into our school.' ... The crowd now let out a roar of rage. 'They've gone in,' a man shouted.

'Oh God,' said a woman, 'the niggers are in school.'

A group of six girls, dressed in skirts and sweaters, hair in pony-tails, started to shriek and wail. 'The niggers are in our school,' they howled hysterically ....

Hysteria swept from the shrieking girls to members of the crowd. Women cried hysterically, tears running down their faces.

Questions

1 Why could it be said that it took even more courage for someone like Zellner (Source 6) to support the Civil Rights Movement than it did for a black person to do so?

2 Why was the CRM more likely to be supported by someone like Robert Zellner, from a well-off white family, than by a white youth from a poor background?

3 Why do you think many black people were beginning to share Williams's views (Source 7)?

4 What is Luther King's main fear if black people respond to attacks by whites with violence of their own (Source 8)?

5 How can you explain the different reactions to the Civil Rights Movement indicated in Sources 6–9?

4.5 Review activity

Which was the biggest threat to democracy in the United States: its treatment of black people or its anti-Communism?

In a democracy, the Government is freely elected by the people after regular elections. An elected government must guarantee certain basic democratic rights, such as freedom of speech, the right to strike, freedom of religion, and fair treatment of all its citizens, no matter what their colour, sex, religion or beliefs. It is clear that during the 1950s in the United States some of these basic rights were denied to both black people and Communists.

In Column 1 of the chart opposite there are eight reasons – four which support the view that ill-treatment of *black people* was the biggest threat to America's democracy, and four suggesting that its ill-treatment of *Communists* was.

America's ill-treatment of its *black population* was the biggest threat to democracy because:	Importance rating for each argument in the first column (0–10, 10 = most important):	I agree/disagree with the argument put forward because:
1 There were far more black people in the USA than Communists. Therefore it was more serious.		
2 Black people could do nothing about the colour of their skin; Communists could always change their views to escape persecution.	4	This isn't the point. People have a right to their opinions and should not have to change them – as long as they don't threaten other people's rights.
3 Black people were often the victims of attacks and murder; Communists were rarely attacked physically.		
4 America's reputation abroad suffered more from its ill-treatment of black people because many other countries were also treating Communists harshly.		

America's ill-treatment of *communists* was the biggest threat to democracy because:	Importance rating for each argument in the first column (0–10, 10 = most important):	I agree/disagree with the argument put forward because:
1 Communists were banned from expressing their views. Freedom of speech is essential for a democracy.	6	Freedom of speech is important but so is the right to eat in the same restaurant or go to the same school as a white. Black people could not do these things; white Communists could.
2 Hysteria about Communism made relations with the Soviet Union even more tense and a war more likely.		
3 Black people were ill-treated illegally by private groups like the KKK; Communists were persecuted by official government policy and so it was more serious.		
4 Communists campaigned for equal rights for black people and fairer treatment for the poor. Without them, the US would have become an even more divided society.		

1 Copy the chart.

2 Fill in Columns 2 and 3. In Column 2, give a mark out of ten for the importance of the reason. In Column 3, give your view of the argument in Column 1, saying whether you agree or disagree with it and why. (An example has been filled in for you.) Try to include some evidence from what you have read in the book so far to back up your views.

Unit 5 • The 1950s: 'Live fast, die young

5.1 Youth rebellion

A new anger

Source 1

Still from the film *The Wild One*, made in 1953. After the film's release, Marlon Brando became a 'role model' for many young people.

■ Why do you think this film was banned in Britain?

In the film *The Wild One*, the actor Marlon Brando plays the tough and angry leader of a leather-jacketed motor-cycle gang. The gang clashes violently with the local townspeople. Asked what he was rebelling against, he replies, 'What've ya got?' In other words, he was rebelling against 'everything'.

The character's reply sums up the general frustration and lack of direction that many young people felt in the 1950s. They wanted to rebel against everything – and especially against whatever their parents believed in. Young people – and teenage boys in particular – formed gangs, cruised in cars, drank heavily and flirted with danger.

Teenage rebellion was a completely new thing. Even the concept of 'teenagers' assumed a new importance. In the past, young adults had simply imitated their parents' tastes and fashions, and had been kept firmly in their place.

What seemed puzzling to those who studied the behaviour and views of these rebellious teenagers was that this rebellion took place at a time when the United States was at its most prosperous.

Source 2

Poster advertising the film *Rebel without a Cause*, 1955.

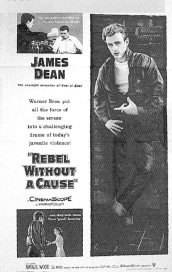

It seemed as though teenagers had taken to heart the words of a novelist of the time, Willard Motley. His finest novel, *We Fished all Night* (1951), tells how a group of teenagers are driven by their slum conditions and poverty into becoming criminals. This quotation from Motley's novel summed up a generation's anger, frustration and search for excitement: 'Live fast, die young, and have a good looking corpse.'

The reckless search for excitement may well have been due, in part, to the fact that American teenagers were the first generation to grow up under the shadow of nuclear war – nuclear weapons could destroy the world at the push of a button. The world may end tomorrow, so why not enjoy it today?

Another reason why teenagers 'rebelled' might be that their parents were looking for safe, quiet lives after the upheavals of the Second World War; this may have made their teenage children want risk and adventure all the more.

The youth film of the 1950s which stands out above all others is *Rebel without a Cause*. Made in 1955, it was actor James Dean's second major film. Dean's character comes to blows with his father, gets into trouble with the police for drunkenness and plays 'chicken run' with a local gang leader, Buzz, in which each drives a car towards a cliff. The loser is the first one to jump out. Buzz is killed as his sleeve catches on the car's door handle. What shocked adults most was the idea that comfortable white middle class families had delinquent children, too!

Dean's death at the age of 24 in 1955, just a few weeks after the film's release, ensured it would become a cult. The manner of his death – a high-speed crash in a sports car – only seemed to reinforce his appeal and the need to 'live fast, die young'.

Why did the youth rebellion shock adults?

In the 1950s, many white middle class parents were shocked and concerned by their teenage children's explosion of anger, and lack of respect for the law. What was it about this youth 'rebellion' which adults found so shocking and so worrying?

'It's only Rock 'n' Roll'

In the 1950s, America's youth discovered 'rock 'n' roll'. This was a new type of music which spread across America and Europe in the 1950s. The music had a strong dance beat, and was dominated by the electric guitar.

Parents hated the new music, and young people could claim it 'belonged' entirely to them. It was a blend of white 'country and western' and black 'rhythm and blues' music styles. (Blues was a type of folk music originating among black Americans at the beginning of the Twentieth century.) For white parents, it was bad enough that 'blues' music was the music of black people, but blues songs were often about what middle class, white Americans considered immoral behaviour. The song 'Young Woman's Blues' in Source 3, by Bessie Smith, the 'Empress of Blues', is one such example.

Source 3

Bessie Smith, 'Young Woman's Blues', 1930s. In the song, the woman, jilted by her lover, does not collapse in a sobbing heap but sets out to find another man.

Woke up this morning when the chickens were crowin' for day,
Looked on the right side of my pillow, my man had gone away.
By the pillow he left a note,
Reading, 'I'm sorry, Jane, you got my goat' –
I'm a young woman, and I ain't done running around.

■ Why might some American parents consider 'Young Woman's Blues' to be unsuitable – especially for teenage girls?

'Old-style' bands, such as 'The Platters', were very different from the 'new-style' rock 'n' rollers. The singer who best represented this apparently 'dangerous' development of rock 'n' roll was Elvis Presley. Presley's thrusting hips and tight trousers horrified parents and delighted teenagers – so much so that some television companies would only film him from the waist up!

Source 4

A 1950s band, 'The Platters'.

Source 5

Elvis Presley.

■ Compare Sources 4 and 5. What was it about Elvis's appearance and manner which might have shocked many adults?

Eddie Cochrane's song 'C'mon Everybody' is revealing. It was a hit in 1959 for the rock 'n' roll singer. It is about teenagers going out for a good time on a Saturday night. Cochrane died in a car crash in 1960.

Source 6

Song by Eddie Cochrane, 'C'mon Everybody', 1959.

Well c'mon everybody
And let's get together tonight
I've got some money in my jeans
And I'm really gonna spend it right
Well, I've been doing my homework all week long
Now the house is empty and my folks are gone
Oh, c'mon everybody!

Well, my baby's number one
But I'm gonna dance with three or four
And the house'll be a-shakin'
From the bare feet a-slappin' on the floor
Well, when you hear the music you can't keep still
If your brother won't rock, then your sister will
Oh, c'mon everybody!

Well, we're gonna have a party
But we'll have to put a guard outside
If the folks come home
They're really gonna have my hide
There'll be no more movies for a week or two
No more runnin' round with the usual crew
Who cares? C'mon everybody!

Jack Gould was a journalist for the *New York Times* – the kind of 'stuffy' newspaper that middle class adults read. He was not fond of rock 'n' roll, as he explains in this extract:

Source 7

Jack Gould in the *New York Times*, 1950s.

delinquent Someone who commits an offence or misdeed – usually a minor one. A 'juvenile delinquent' was a young person with anti-social and troublesome behaviour.

These gyrations [of Elvis's hips] have to concern parents unless we're the kind of parents who approve of kids going around stealing hubcaps, indulging in promiscuity [easy sex] and generally behaving like delinquents* ... it isn't enough to say that Elvis is kind to his parents, sends money home and is the same unspoilt kid as before all the commotion began. That still isn't a free ticket to behave like a sex maniac in public before millions of impressionable kids.

Journalists like Gould (Source 7) blamed rock 'n' roll for the increase in delinquent behaviour, but others were but not convinced by this argument. A modern writer, Chris Pearce, discusses the rise in youth crime in the 1950s in Source 8.

Source 8

From Chris Pearce, *The Fifties*, 1991.

... juvenile delinquency was a serious social problem, and one which statistics showed was getting worse in the course of the decade. For example, the summer of 1956 produced a 26 per cent increase in possession of dangerous weapons. Teenagers became universally branded with the delinquent image. 'I'm not a Juvenile Delinquent' sang Frankie Lymon and the Teenagers in the 1957 film *Rock Rock Rock*. Lymon himself was only 15 years old, but a year later started the drug habit that killed him in 1968.

[However] juvenile delinquency existed before rock 'n' roll ....

Questions

1. What does the journalist dislike about Elvis Presley (Source 7)?

2. What might Gould's reaction be to Source 6? Explain your answer.

3. Does the author of Source 8 suggest that rock 'n' roll was the cause of juvenile delinquency? Explain your answer.

4. Would your view of Source 8 be any different if the last sentence were not included ('Juvenile delinquency existed before rock 'n' roll')?

5. Could the views of the writer in Source 8 be used to support those of Jack Gould in Source 7? Give reasons for your answer.

6. How do Sources 5–8 help to explain the shock and concern of many parents about the behaviour of their teenage children?

5.2 Women after the war: a decade of frustration?

The 'ideal home-maker'

After the Second World War there was a return to more conventional roles for women, though the number of women workers did continue to increase from the late 1940s onwards. The average age at which women got married in 1950 was 20 – the youngest since 1890. Articles in magazines and newspapers encouraged women to return to the home and to their traditional roles as wives, mothers and housewives. Source 1 shows the kind of advice that one publication of the 1950s gave its readers:

Source 1

The Woman's Guide to Better Living, 1950s.

■ How might a working woman feel about this statement?

Whether you are a man or a woman, the family is the unit to which you most genuinely belong .... The family is the centre of your living. If it isn't, you've gone astray.

Women who went out to work, especially those with full-time careers, were regarded with suspicion. A very influential book of the 1950s was *Modern Women: the Lost Sex* by Marynia Farnham and Ferdinand Lundgren. The authors blamed the problems of modern society – such as alcoholism, teenage hooliganism and even war – on 'neurotic' career women. They claimed that these women abandoned the care of their children to others and pointlessly competed with men, so adding to the aggression in the world.

If the woman's place was in the kitchen, the 'American Dream' meant having the very best and the newest gadgets for the home:

Source 2

Advertisement for kitchen equipment, 1952. It shows a kitchen so modern and easy to use that even men are happy to work in it!

However, growing numbers of women in the 1950s – and middle class women in particular – began to reject these views. In the 1960s many thousands joined feminist organisations such as the National Organisation for Women (NOW). What made these women dissatisfied with their lives?

Why did many women become feminists?

By the early 1960s there was a growing reaction against the traditional idea of home-making. Many women decided that there was more to life than babies, sparkling dishes and happy husbands. Some women remembered how in the 1940s they had done vital and demanding work in the Second World War. Their contribution had been important and their jobs valued and valuable.

This account by a modern historian summarises what women began to question about their lives:

Source 3

J. P. Diggins, *The Proud Decades*, 1989.

Marriage was celebrated as a state of bliss. So, too, was having children. In diaper [nappy] ads babies always smiled and never cried .... Indeed, housewifely tasks were glorified as proof of the 'complete' woman: chef, hostess, nurse, laundress, maid, story-teller, shopper, PTA [Parent Teacher Association] member, flower-planter, interior-decorator ....

A key factor in this reaction was Betty Friedan, a psychologist who had given up her career for marriage and a family. In 1963 she wrote an influential book called *The Feminine Mystique*. In it she said that women had been conditioned into believing that motherhood and home-making were the highest achievements they should aim for in life.

Source 4

Betty Friedan, *The Feminine Mystique*, 1963.

■ How do Friedan's views contrast with those expressed in Source 1?

The problem lay buried, unspoken for many years in the minds of American women. It was a strange stirring, a sense of dissatisfaction, a yearning that women suffered in the middle of the Twentieth century in the United States.

Each suburban wife struggled with it alone as she made the beds, shopped for groceries, matched slip cover material, ate peanut butter sandwiches, chauffeured Cub Scouts and Brownies, lay beside her husband at night. She was afraid to ask even of herself the silent question: 'Is this all?' ... We can no longer ignore the voice within women that says: 'I want something more than my husband and my children and my home.'

Betty Friedan called on women to reject this 'mystique' and to develop themselves through education and work outside the home. She suggested that men and women should raise their families as equal partners, sharing responsibilities in a sort of 'business partnership'. The book was important because it expressed the frustration of many women who felt trapped in the traditional role of housewife. It also helped to pave the way for the Women's Movement of the 1960s.

The spread of the suburbs

One new development of the 1950s was the suburb. Many middle class families abandoned the centre of cities for life in new homes in the suburbs. These houses were usually moderately priced, so that newly married couples could afford them. One writer of the time, Lewis Mumford, was hostile to the spread of these suburbs:

Source 5

Lewis Mumford, *The City in History*, 1961.

In the mass movement into suburban areas a new kind of community was produced ... identical, unidentifiable houses, lined up endlessly at identical distances, on identical roads, in a treeless wasteland, inhabited by people in the same class, the same income, the same age group, watching the same television programmes, eating the same tasteless pre-fabricated foods from the same freezers ....

Many women, isolated and bored in their new suburban homes, looked for companionship in the weekly 'Tupperware party'. Women would meet together over a cup of coffee to buy kitchen products made by Tupperware.

Source 6

Housewives meeting at a 'Tupperware party' in the 1950s.

Questions

1 What was the reason for the frustration felt by women, described in Source 4?

2 Why might the life described in Source 5 be particularly depressing for women?

3 Do you think events such as the 'Tupperware party' in Source 6 would have done much to improve the lives of suburban housewives? Explain your answer.

4 War work in industry had never been especially popular with middle class women during the war. Look back at Rosie the Riveter in Source 7, page 63. Why might women of the 1950s have a different view of the image shown in this source?

5 What do Sources 1–6 tell us about the problems which women faced in the 1950s?

5.3 The affluent Fifties?

An age of mass-consumption

The statistics of the 1950s tell of a rich America getting richer still. Each year industry produced and sold more goods, inflation was low, and workers' real incomes rose steadily. By 1960, the average worker had about 40 per cent more to spend in real terms than he or she had in 1949.

There were several reasons for this boom. It was partly the result of Americans spending the $100 billion they had saved during the Second World War. Much of this money went on consumer goods, with televisions, refrigerators, freezers and cars leading the way.

Another reason for the boom was the improved efficiency of the workforce. This meant that goods could be produced more cheaply, and that kept the prices down. The growth in the population, from 151 million in 1950 to 179 million in 1960, was a further reason. All these factors led to more demand for goods.

Finally, the Korean War (1950–1953) and the ongoing Cold War meant that American industries were kept busy turning out new weapons for the defence of the country. This meant big orders for industries like steel, coal and electronics.

How prosperous were people in the 1950s?

In the post-war period, the USA experienced a huge boom. But did *all* Americans benefit? Did everyone become wealthier?

The table below shows the ownership of three common consumer goods – cars, televisions and refrigerators. Generally speaking, the greater the number of families owning these items, the higher the standard of living of the population.

Source 1

Post-war Economic Trends in the United States, edited by R. Freeman, 1960.

■ Which item shows the greatest increase? Why do you think this is?

Standard of living in the USA, 1946–1956

| Year | Percentage of families owning | | |
	Cars (%)	TV (%)	Fridges (%)
1946	Not available	0	69
1951	65	38.5	87
1956	73	81	96

Unemployment figures are a key indicator of people's prosperity. The numbers of those out of work, though, are of little use unless we know what percentage of the adult population they make up. The higher the percentage is, the greater the overall poverty. Remember that in 1933, at the worst point of the Great Depression, the percentage of unemployed stood at 25 per cent.

Source 2

Statistical Abstract of the United States, 1971.

Unemployment in the USA, 1946–1960

Year	Unemployed (millions)	Adult population without work (%)
1946	2.3	3.9
1948	2.1	3.4
1950	3.1	5.0
1952	1.7	2.7
1954	3.2	5.0
1956	2.6	3.8
1958	4.7	6.8
1960	3.9	5.6

The number of people living below the poverty line is another useful indicator of how prosperous people are:

Source 3

Statistics from US Department of Commerce, 1959.

People living in poverty in the USA, 1959

Racial group	Below poverty line (millions)	Below poverty line (%)
All groups	39.5	22
Whites	28.5	18
Blacks	11.0	56

This advertisement features a family who have just bought a new car – a Plymouth. The advertisers clearly have in mind the kind of family which can afford their product.

Source 4

Advertisment for a Plymouth car, 1950s.

▮ In what ways is this supposed to be the traditional family?

"Oh, Boy! It's Pop with a new PLYMOUTH!"

A modern historian writes about what the 1950s meant to middle class families who wanted to have the latest and the best products available:

Source 5

J. P. Diggins, *The Proud Decades*, 1989.

Americans junked almost as many cars as Detroit made ... and rushed out to buy the latest novelty, whether it was a convertible [car with a soft roof], TV set, deep-freeze, electric carving knife, or the 'New Look' Christian Dior evening dress .... Immediately after the war, household appliances were in demand, then luxuries like fashionable clothes and imported wines. For those who bought homes for $8,000 or more, luxuries were seen as necessities. The middle-class suburb dweller looked out of his window and 'needed' what his neighbour had – a white Corvette [sports car] or a swimming pool.

In 1962, Michael Harrington (see page 75) wrote about how a Welfare Office treated applicants for social security benefits during the 1950s:

Source 6

M. Harrington, *The Other America*, 1962.

They regarded most of those who came to them as 'deadbeats' and 'bums', and they were determined to keep freeloaders from getting state benefits. As a result, they rejected 55 per cent of applicants, and they were quite proud of it and determined to keep it there.

To a person from the middle class, the fact that documents are required by a public agency seems obvious and sensible. Yet this misses a basic fact about the poor generally, and the aged poor in particular: that they are the ones least able to deal with the form-filling bureaucracy of the welfare state. Some of the American poor have difficulty with the English language, and almost all of them are undereducated.

Questions

1 Which of Sources 1–6 suggest that Americans became richer after the Second World War? Explain your answer.

2 Which of Sources 1–6 suggest that some Americans were not so well-off by the end of the 1950s? Explain your answer.

3 Source 3 gives statistics only for 1959. How would figures before and after that year give a fuller picture of poverty in the United States?

4 Does Source 4 tell us anything useful about the prosperity of Americans in the 1950s? Explain your answer.

5 The historian in Source 5 has written an inaccurate account of the 1950s because it does not agree with the other accounts in Sources 1–6. Explain whether you agree with this view or not.

5.4 Review activity

How far did the position of women change between 1933 and 1963?

This chart looks at the position of women from 1933 to 1963. Your task is to assess just how much things changed for women in this period in the four areas listed in Column 1. You will need to refer back to Unit 2 as well as to Section 5.2 to help you complete the activity.

Area	1933–1940	1941–1945	1946–1963
1 Women in the economy (e.g. jobs, pay)			
2 Social attitudes to women	Nothing much changed for women in this period. It was still generally accepted that women's chief role was in the home, looking after the family.		
3 Women's ideas about themselves	A few women became public figures in exciting areas such as sport and aviation, but most women accepted a more traditional role in the home.		
4 Social and economic position of black women		Black women did find some new opportunities in the armed forces, but were segregated from white women in the same way as black men were segregated.	

1 Copy the chart above.

2 Complete the three columns. (Three of the boxes have already been filled in for you, but you are welcome to change or add to them.)

Unit 6 · Kennedy: a 'New Frontier'?

John F. Kennedy became America's youngest President in 1961 at the age of 43. He was a glamorous leader – attractive, wealthy, well-educated, witty, and married to a beautiful and cultured woman, Jacqueline Lee Bouvier (Source 1). He had been decorated as a war hero while commanding a torpedo boat in the Pacific in the Second World War, and the episode was later made into a film, *PT 109*.

Source 1

Jacqueline Bouvier Kennedy, wife of the President, was a great political asset to him, and he was keen to be photographed with her.

Kennedy would need all of these advantages if he was to make a success of the task which faced him. He inherited an America where unemployment

Source 2

Kennedy's children were the youngest in the twentieth century to live in the White House. The President was keen to let the public see them in informal situations, as this official photograph shows.

■ Why do you think Kennedy was so keen to have his children photographed at the White House?

was increasing – there were more than twice as many people unemployed in 1961 as there had been in the early 1950s – and youth was in angry mood. Growing numbers of women were frustrated about their role in society, and black people resented the fact that the government seemed to do little and care little about their problems.

The United States abroad faced a Communist Soviet Union whose military might was, Americans thought, equal or even greater than its own. Its leader, Nikita Khrushchev, seemed keen to show the USA its strength and flaunt its nuclear potential.

When Kennedy was assassinated in November 1963, three years after being elected President, how much had changed? How successful was he as President? Historians' views of Kennedy's short presidency have varied greatly. Some historians have bitterly condemned Kennedy; others have celebrated the charismatic leader. Their view of him has also been influenced by his dramatic assassination in 1963, and the myth that grew up around him (see pages 109–110). It is hard to be completely objective when the end of his presidency was so sudden and tragic.

In domestic affairs, Kennedy's record was mixed. Under his presidency, the American economy had prospered, and industrial output had increased. By 1963, unemployment had come down a little, but still stood at just over 4 million – 6 per cent of the population. There were fewer black people (51 per cent) and white (19.5 per cent) living below the poverty line than in 1959 (see Source 3, page 92 for a comparison with the 1959 figure).

However, it is interesting to note that in the next three years under President Johnson, there was a remarkable drop of over 20 per cent (to 40 per cent of the black population in 1966) in the number of black people below the poverty line – twice the fall achieved by Kennedy in the same length of time.

The following table shows America's Gross National Product between 1952 and 1963. GNP is a measure of the wealth a country produces. The GNP for the Eisenhower presidency is given for comparison.

Source 3

1 What general trend can be seen from these figures?

2 Compare the last three years of Eisenhower's presidency (1958–1960) with the three years of Kennedy's presidency (1961–1963). Is there any significant difference in the increase in GNP between the two periods?

Gross National Product (GNP), 1952–1963

Year	GNP (in $ billions)	Year	GNP (in $ billions)
1952	347	1958	444
1953	365	1959	482
1954	363	1960	502
1955	397	1961	518
1956	419	1962	554
1957	443	1963	583

In 1963, women had begun to find a voice of their own, and the Women's Movement was beginning to take shape. There had been some small improvements in the legal and political position of black people but nothing really substantial. What black people may have found in Kennedy, though, was someone in the White House who did at least seem to *care* about their situation, even if he did little to change it.

By 1963, efforts to improve education, provide health insurance and address the problems of poverty in cities had not been particularly successful. They had been blocked by the conservative Democrats in Congress.

In military terms, the United States was a much greater power, and one which easily outstripped the Soviet Union in nuclear weapons. Kennedy had shown firmness with the USSR, forcing the Soviet leader, Khrushchev, to back down over Cuba in 1962. By 1963, the United States was clearly the world's dominant power.

6.1 Kennedy and American society

The new President: a mixed reaction

In the 1960 presidential election the two candidates were Richard Nixon, the Republican, and the less well-known Democrat, John Kennedy. During the campaign, Kennedy scored great successes in his television debates with Nixon in front of huge national audiences. The younger man had more poise in front of the cameras, and he leapt ahead in the polls as a result of his regular TV appearances.

Kennedy's election campaign also featured the usual meet-the-people tours. Being seen with ordinary people was vital for an upper class politician like Kennedy. His privileged background counted against him with some voters.

Source 1

Kennedy campaigning for the presidential election, 1960.

Nearly 69 million votes were cast in the election. The Democratic candidate, John F. Kennedy, won 34,227,000 of them; his Republican opponent, Richard Nixon, polled 34,107,000. It was the narrowest of victories for Kennedy.

Kennedy aroused mixed reactions. Some people hated him because he came from a rich, upper class family, and they believed that his father had 'bought' him political success. Some believed that his willingness to seek agreement with the Soviet Union and to sell it wheat as a gesture of friendship meant that he was 'soft on Communism'. He was particularly hated in the South because he was a Northerner who sympathised with the plight of black people.

Critics were not slow to show their feelings towards Kennedy. The political jokes in Source 2 were told during his presidency. The first joke relates to an incident in the Second World War. During the war, Kennedy served on a motor torpedo boat (PT 109) which was sliced in half and sunk by a Japanese destroyer in the Pacific. Southern cinema-goers obviously had their own reasons for wanting to see the film!

Source 2

Popular jokes of the 1960s, quoted in W. Manchester, *The Glory and the Dream*, 1973.

■ Explain the point of each of the three anti-Kennedy jokes.

The sign on the marquee outside a Georgia theatre showing [the film] *PT 109*, the story of the President's World War II heroism, read 'See how the Japs almost got Kennedy'.

A riddle ran, 'If Jack [John Kennedy], Bobby [Robert Kennedy] and Teddy [Edward Kennedy] were on a sinking boat, who would be saved?' The answer: 'The country'.

[A] widely circulated leaflet set forth plans for a Kennedy monument in Washington: 'It was thought unwise to place it beside that of George Washington, who never told a lie, nor beside that of F. D. Roosevelt, who never told the truth, since John [Kennedy] cannot tell the difference.'

For some people, on the other hand, Kennedy was an inspiring speaker and charismatic leader. He had great charm. And he offered hope for a good future in an uncertain world of Cold War.

A new frontier?

In his acceptance speech as Democratic candidate, Kennedy promised the American people a 'New Frontier':

Source 3

Extract from Kennedy's acceptance speech, 1960.

We stand at the edge of a New Frontier – the frontier of unknown opportunities and perils – a frontier of unfulfilled hopes and dreams .... [The New Frontier would deal with] unsolved problems of peace and war, unconquered pockets of ignorance and prejudice, unanswered questions of poverty and surplus.

But in the speech he made on the day he became President, Kennedy said:

Source 4

Kennedy's speech on the day he was made President in January 1961 was full of powerful images, as this extract shows.

'The torch has been passed to a new generation of Americans – born in this century, tempered [strengthened] by war, disciplined by a hard and bitter peace .... [The speech asked Americans] to pay any price, bear any burden, meet any hardship, support any friend, oppose any foe to assure the survival and the success of liberty.

These were inspiring words that made clear where Kennedy's main interests would be: in foreign affairs. But what did he do, in the field of internal affairs, to cross the new frontier announced only a year before?

Kennedy and civil rights

Kennedy may have been concerned about civil rights for black people, but he knew that any serious effort to ensure justice for black Americans would cost him the support of Southern Democrats in Congress.

At that time, Congress was controlled by Republicans and conservative

Southern Democrats. Kennedy would need the Democrats' support to get his own proposals accepted by Congress. The prejudice against black people was particularly strong in the Southern states, and any Southern politician who supported civil rights for blacks risked losing white votes and his seat in Congress.

President Kennedy did not play a leading role in the Civil Rights Movement. However, he did send troops to the University of Mississippi in the autumn of 1962 so that a black student, James Meredith, could take up his studies. It confirmed the trend of the 1950s that the Federal Government would get involved in, and undermine if necessary, the rights of the individual states. It also meant that, by the summer of 1963, Alabama was the only state with a segregated education system. The Governor of Alabama, George Wallace, finally gave in that summer and allowed desegregation.

A new bill for civil rights

Eventually, in February 1963, Kennedy decided the time had come to propose a Civil Rights Bill to Congress. This would give black people equality in public housing and education, and would end discrimination in any government-funded schemes. However, the Bill made little progress in Congress as opponents continually raised objections to it. In August, the black leader Martin Luther King led a march of 200,000 through Washington in support of the Bill, but it was rejected by Congress.

Kennedy had asked King to call off the march while his Civil Rights Bill was being debated by Congress. Kennedy told King that some members of Congress were looking for an excuse to oppose the Bill, claiming they would not vote for it 'at the point of a gun'. King refused and suggested that if it was called off it could lead more militant black people to use violence.

Source 5

Civil rights march in support of the new Bill, 1963. Martin Luther King is seen here, fourth from the left, leading 200,000 black protesters to Washington.

1 What are the campaigners demanding on their placards?

2 Why do you think Kennedy believed that the march would harm the chances of the Civil Rights Bill being approved?

Kennedy's assassination in November 1963 brought about a dramatic change in the attitude of Congress as a wave of sympathy for the dead President swept the country. A tougher version of the Bill, giving black people greater rights in voting, was finally passed in 1964 under Kennedy's successor as President, Lyndon Johnson.

Kennedy and others believed that the civil rights issue was a major cause of his problems with Congress, as Source 6 makes clear. It concerns a conversation between the leader of the Democrats in Congress, Carl Albert, and Kennedy in June 1963 – the day after a NAACP leader, Medgar Evers, had been murdered.

Source 6

Taylor Branch, *Parting the Waters: Martin Luther King and the Civil Rights Movement 1954–63*, 1988.

■ Why do you think Albert felt he had to apologise for the failure of some Democrats to support Kennedy's Bill for public works?

On the morning after the Evers murder, Majority Leader Carl Albert called President Kennedy to apologise for those Democrats who had voted against and defeated a $450 million section of the Kennedy Administration's public works bill. 'I couldn't do a damn thing with them, you know,' said Albert, and the President instantly understood.

'Civil rights did it,' Kennedy replied ... 'Christ you know, it's like they shoot this guy [Evers] in Mississippi ... I mean, it's just in everything.'

Albert agreed that the civil rights uproar was 'overwhelming the whole programme.'

On every close question from foreign aid to the space budget, civil rights loomed as the cause of defeat.

Help for the poor and sick

Kennedy's ambitious programme to provide medical care for the old (known as 'Medicare') and to provide federal money for state education was rejected by Congress. Once again, these measures would be passed only after his assassination.

There were some successes for Kennedy while he lived, though. The minimum wage was increased to $1.25 an hour, some money was spent to improve housing in poor areas, and the period for which unemployment benefit could be paid was increased.

Questions

1 Why was Kennedy reluctant to get too involved in the campaign for black civil rights?

2 What progress towards civil rights for black people was made during Kennedy's presidency?

3 The Bill which was defeated on this occasion concerned government plans to build new roads and housing. Why, therefore, is it surprising that it was rejected by Congress?

4 Why do you think Congress was willing to support Kennedy's proposals after his assassination?

5 Why did Kennedy find it so difficult to change American society?

6.2 Kennedy and Cuba, 1961–1962

Kennedy's success in foreign affairs was likewise mixed. His biggest challenge – and the most dangerous one – came from Cuba, an island in the Caribbean some 150 km south of Florida. Two crises in relations between Cuba and the United States, one in 1961 and the other in 1962, took the world to the brink of a nuclear war..

Since becoming independent from Spain in 1898, Cuba had been strongly influenced by the United States. Americans owned over 80 per cent of the island's mines, oil refineries and cattle ranches, and 40 per cent of its sugar industry. In 1952 a dictator, Batista, supported by the United States, took power. His government was corrupt and unpopular.

Castro takes power in Cuba

In 1959, a tiny guerrilla force of just 800, led by Fidel Castro, overthrew Batista. Castro became Prime Minister in Cuba. Though he welcomed Russian support, he was not, at this time, a Communist. He was basically a nationalist, and his main aim was to free Cuba from American economic control to provide poor Cubans with a better standard of living. He introduced a series of reforms to improve the lives of ordinary Cubans. He also confiscated over a million acres of land from American companies. Many wealthier Cubans fled into exile in the USA.

US anger grew further when Castro confiscated American oil companies operating in Cuba and brought them under Cuban ownership. The US Government retaliated by refusing to buy 700,000 tonnes of Cuban sugar. This was a vital source of income for the Cubans and it would have wrecked their economy. The Russians offered to buy it all. This was the last straw for the President at the time, Eisenhower. It seemed that Cuba was on the verge of becoming a Communist state.

The 'Bay of Pigs' affair

In the spring of 1960, President Eisenhower gave permission to the US Central Intelligence Agency (CIA) to train anti-Castro Cubans living in the United States for an invasion of their homeland, Cuba. The plan was that as soon as the 1,500 anti-Castro Cubans arrived in the Bay of Pigs, the population of Cuba would join them and overthrow the 'unpopular' Castro. American involvement would never be revealed.

In fact, the scheme was very poorly planned from the start, and unlikely to succeed. However, Kennedy took over the plan when he became President, and gave his approval for it.

Source 1

The Bay of Pigs in Cuba. This was where the anti-Castro Cuban exiles landed and launched their ill-fated attack.

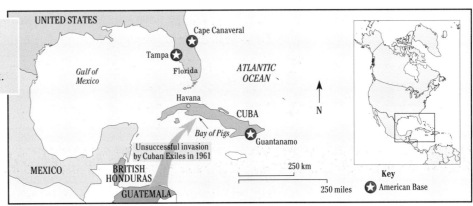

1 How close is Cuba to the United States?

2 Why would it have made more military sense to launch the attack from Florida? What political reason was there not to do this?

The CIA-trained force landed in the Bay of Pigs in Cuba on 17 April 1961. Things went wrong from the start. The hulls of the landing craft were ripped open by what the CIA reconnaissance photographs had shown to be seaweed. The 'seaweed' turned out to be razor sharp reefs. The invasion was supported briefly by unmarked US Navy jets; four of the American pilots were killed, along with 114 anti-Castro Cubans.

The invasion was a disaster, and 1,200 anti-Castro Cubans were captured. Kennedy refused to send in US troops or order further attacks by US aircraft. Most importantly, the Cuban population did *not* support the rebellion, and the invasion attempt failed miserably.

Results of the 'Bay of Pigs' affair

The consequences of the affair were significant. The Cuban people had not overthrown Fidel Castro. Instead, Cuba drew *closer* to Communist Russia. Khrushchev, the Soviet leader, began shipping weapons to the Cubans as Cuba adopted more and more Communist policies. Khrushchev was convinced that the young and inexperienced Kennedy could easily be outsmarted.

This was to cause an even more serious crisis the following year when the Soviet leader decided that Kennedy could be bullied into allowing the USSR to supply nuclear missiles to Cuba. But first, in August 1961, a separate crisis in US–Soviet relations flared up in Berlin.

The Berlin Wall, 1961

The Communist government of East Germany decided that it had to do something to stop the flow of its most qualified citizens from East Berlin into West Berlin. Many East Germans wanted to escape Communist rule and flee to a freer and more prosperous life in the West. Incredibly, the East Germans, with Krushchev's backing, built a wall that completely surrounded West Berlin, so that East Germans could no longer get into the western part of the city.

Kennedy was quick to visit West Berlin after the wall, complete with barbed wire running along the top, had been built around it. He reassured West Berliners that the United States and the West would not abandon them. In a rousing speech, he said:

Source 2

This cartoon is from the humorous British magazine, *Punch*, September 1961. It sums up *Punch's* view of American–Soviet relations.

VITAL DISCUSSION

■ What does the cartoon suggest about American–Soviet relations in September 1961?

Source 3

Speech by J. F. Kennedy in Berlin, June 1962.

■ What do you suppose Kennedy meant by the phrase, 'Let them come to Berlin!'?

There are many people in the world who really don't understand, or say they don't, what is the great issue between the free world and the Communist world. Let them come to Berlin! There are some who say that Communism is the wave of the future. Let them come to Berlin! ... All free men, wherever they may live, are citizens of Berlin, and therefore, as a free man, I take pride in the words: 'Ich bin ein Berliner!' [I am a Berliner].

Though tension between the Communist bloc and the West increased, the building of the wall actually came as something of a relief – the USA had feared there might be a Soviet invasion of West Berlin. As Kennedy said, 'A wall is a hell of a lot better than a war.' However, it was a defeat for Kennedy and the West as their grip on West Berlin was even more threatened. It made Kennedy more determined to show Khrushchev that the United States would not be bullied by the Soviet Union.

'Eyeball to eyeball' over Cuba

Khrushchev was convinced by the Bay of Pigs that Kennedy was a weak leader. He began shipping nuclear weapons into Cuba. Fidel Castro, resenting the USA after the attempted invasion at the Bay of Pigs, allowed the Soviet Union to install the missile launching pads on the island. These were soon identified by US reconnaissance planes in October 1962. For the first time, every major US city was within striking distance of a Soviet nuclear missile.

Source 4

Soviet nuclear missile sites in Cuba, 1962. This photograph was taken by an American reconnaissance plane. The Russians must have known that their missile sites could easily be identified from the air.

■ Can you think of any reason why they seemed to make little effort to conceal their missiles?

Kennedy faced three options. He could order an air strike against the missile sites in Cuba and risk a war; he could order an invasion of Cuba and almost certainly start a nuclear war; or he could try to negotiate his way out of the crisis by persuading the Soviet Union to pull out its missiles.

He decided on the last option, and meanwhile strengthened America's position by setting up a naval blockade, or 'quarantine', around Cuba. This was to stop and search any Soviet cargo ships approaching the island. US troops were sent down to the south-eastern states and Polaris nuclear submarines put to sea.

Would the Russians allow their cargo ships to be searched or would they resist? The world seemed on the brink of a war as 25 Russian vessels sailed towards Cuba.

Source 5

The nuclear missile threat, 1962. This map shows the ranges of the missiles installed in Cuba. The 'quarantine', or isolation, of Cuba meant that Soviet ships approaching the island would have to be stopped by the US Navy.

■ Why do you think Americans were so concerned about these particular missiles?

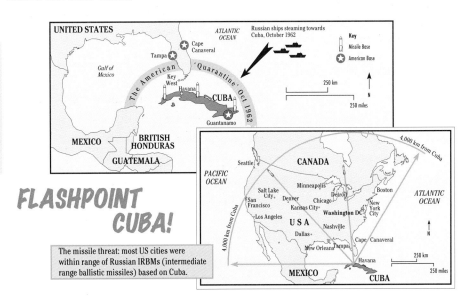

FLASHPOINT CUBA!

The missile threat: most US cities were within range of Russian IRBMs (intermediate range ballistic missiles) based on Cuba.

On 25 October Khrushchev ordered the ships to turn back. Dean Rusk, Kennedy's Secretary of State for Foreign Affairs, commented: 'We're eyeball to eyeball and I think the other fellow just blinked.' But the crisis was not over. Khrushchev demanded that the Americans withdraw their missiles from Turkey (an American NATO ally on Russia's border) and then the Russians would pull their missiles out of Cuba.

This was a difficult issue for Kennedy. He had secretly ordered those missiles to be withdrawn before the crisis began, but if he agreed now it would look as if he was giving in to Khrushchev. Kennedy decided to ignore Khrushchev's demand. Instead it was the Soviet leader who backed down. On 28 October Khrushchev agreed to remove the existing nuclear weapons from Cuba. Kennedy, for his part, promised not to invade Cuba but said nothing about the missiles in Turkey. It was quite a victory for Kennedy.

Relations between the Soviet Union and the United States improved after the crisis. Both countries realised how close they had come to war. They agreed to set up a direct telephone link between their leaders to communicate more quickly in times of crisis, and in 1963 both countries signed the Nuclear Test Ban Treaty against nuclear tests in the atmosphere.

Source 6

Cartoon on the missile crisis from the British newspaper, the *Daily Mail*, October 1962. The character in black on the horse is Khrushchev while the figure on the donkey is Castro. Kennedy is on the left.

■ How does this British cartoon make clear its support for Kennedy?

Questions

1 What did Dean Rusk mean by the sentence, 'We're eyeball to eyeball and I think the other fellow just blinked.' (above)? Do you think it is an appropriate description of the crisis?

2 Some critics of Kennedy have argued that he risked a nuclear war with the Soviet Union just so he would not lose face as he had over the Bay of Pigs. What is your view?

3 At which stage in the crisis do you think the Soviet Union and the United States were closest to war? Explain your answer.

4 What do you think was the turning point of the crisis, after which war was unlikely? Explain your answer.

6.3 The assassination of Kennedy

The news that stunned the world

On 22 November 1963, Kennedy decided to visit Dallas, Texas, to win the support of Southern Democrats for his policies. On the morning of his visit he read the *Dallas Morning News* which accused him of giving in to Moscow, and demanded to know why American Communists were such keen supporters of Kennedy. He did not expect a warm welcome.

Kennedy decided to travel through the city in an open-topped limousine with his wife, Jacqueline, sitting next to him and the Governor of Texas, John Connally, and his wife in front. As the presidential motorcade entered Dealey Plaza and drove along Elm Street, Kennedy was struck by at least two bullets. One of these blew away twelve square centimetres of his skull and killed him instantly.

A man, Lee Harvey Oswald, was arrested that day and accused of having shot Kennedy from the sixth floor of the Texas School Book Depository Building. Two days later Oswald was himself shot and killed by Jack Ruby, a Dallas nightclub owner.

Was there a conspiracy to kill JFK?

Source 1

Artist's reconstruction of the scene of Kennedy's assassination.

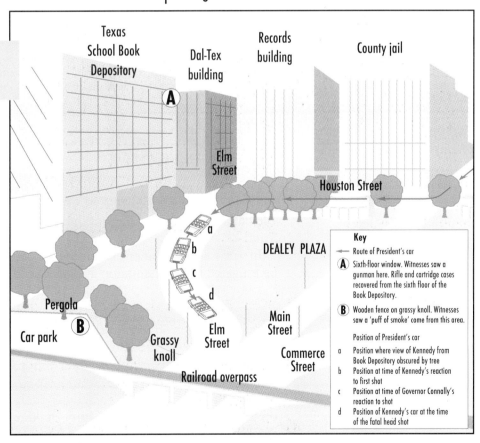

Source 1 is a drawing of Dealey Plaza where Kennedy was shot. Lee Harvey Oswald, it was claimed, fired three shots from the position marked A. However, some witnesses claimed that at least one shot was fired from the position marked B. If this is true, there must have been *two* gunmen involved, and therefore there was a 'conspiracy'.

The mystery of who killed Kennedy and why has baffled people for decades. The assassination is a good example of the problems historians face in trying to assess the evidence available. There is a great deal of evidence about the killing – unfortunately much of it is contradictory.

The lack of conclusive evidence has left historians with many unanswered questions. Did Oswald kill Kennedy? If so, why? Was he part of a conspiracy? Were there two or more gunmen? How many shots were fired? Was Jack Ruby acting alone, or was he paid to silence Oswald before he could reveal the truth?

A key issue is whether there was a conspiracy to kill Kennedy. He had made many enemies. The Mafia had good reason to want Kennedy dead. Robert Kennedy, the President's brother, was the US Attorney-General and had been leading a strong campaign against the Mafia. Southern racists had been angered by Kennedy's support for civil rights for black people. The CIA had a motive, too. Kennedy had stopped listening to the CIA after the Bay of Pigs disaster and it resented being cold-shouldered by the President.

Were any of these powerful groups involved in killing the President? If there was a conspiracy, it would cause a huge political crisis to unravel it.

Source 2

A reconstruction of the assassination. It shows Kennedy in the telescopic sights of a rifle.

■ Look at the map of Dealey Plaza (Source 1). Was the gunman in this reconstruction firing from the Texas School Book Depository or from the grassy knoll? Explain your answer.

There have been two official investigations into the assassination – in 1964 and 1976. The findings of the two investigations are given in Sources 3 and 4.

In 1964 a Government Commission, led by Chief Justice Earl Warren, investigated the assassination and produced these conclusions:

Source 3

Report of the Warren Commission, 1964.

The shots which killed President Kennedy were fired from the sixth floor window ... of the Texas School Book Depository. This determination [conclusion] is based on the following:
(a) The nearly whole bullet found on Governor Connally's stretcher ...[was} fired from the 6.5-millimeter Mannlicher-Carcano rifle found on the sixth floor of the Depository Building ....
(b) The three used cartridge cases found near the window of the sixth floor were fired from the same rifle which fired the above bullet ....
(c) The windshield in the presidential limousine was struck by a bullet fragment on the inside surface of the glass, but was not penetrated.

(d) The nature of the wounds suffered by President Kennedy and Governor Connally and the location of the car ... establish that the bullets were fired from above and behind the presidential limousine ... striking the President ... as follows:

President Kennedy was first struck by a bullet which entered the back of his neck and exited through the lower front portion of his neck, causing a wound which would not necessarily have been lethal. The President was struck a second time by a bullet which entered the right-rear portion of his head, causing a massive and fatal wound ....

There is no credible [believable] evidence that the shots were fired from the Triple Underpass, ahead of the motorcade, or from any other direction ....

On the basis of the evidence before the Commission it concludes that Oswald acted alone.

In 1976 the Senate set up a committee to reopen the investigation of the assassination. There was some new evidence in the form of a policeman's motor-cycle tape recording which suggested that four shots were fired. There was also a general feeling that the Warren Commission had disregarded evidence if it contradicted their conclusion that Oswald acted alone.

The Senate Select Committee completed its investigation in 1979. This is a summary of its key findings:

Source 4

Report of the Select Committee on Assassinations, 1979.

Lee Harvey Oswald fired three shots at President ... Kennedy. The second and third shots he fired struck the President. The third shot he fired killed the President. The shots that struck President Kennedy from behind were fired from the sixth floor window of the Texas School Book Depository building. Scientific acoustical evidence [sound recording] establishes a high probability that two gunmen fired at President Kennedy. A newly-found tape recording of a motor-cycle policeman's radio transmission has shown that four, not three, shots were fired. Very sophisticated electronic analysis of the tape also suggests that one of the shots was fired from a small grassy hill in front of the motorcade.

The Committee believes ... that President Kennedy was probably assassinated as a result of a conspiracy. The Committee is unable to identify the other gunmen or the extent of the conspiracy.

Doubts were also raised about the accuracy of the weapon used by Oswald – not to mention his ability as a marksman.

Lee Harvey Oswald had been a marine but his marksmanship record was only average. The rifle he used was a Second World War Italian bolt action rifle. Each individual shot required the assassin to pull back a bolt and then find the target again through the telescopic sight. The rifle also had a recoil which means that it 'kicked back' after firing. The Senate Committee established that all four shots were fired within 8.3 seconds and that the third and fourth shot were fired less than a second apart.

Questions

1   Was there a conspiracy?

	Warren Commission 1964	Select Committee 1979
1 How many shots were fired?		
2 Were all the shots fired from the School Book Depository Building?		No. One shot was fired from the grassy knoll in front of the motorcade.
3 Was Kennedy killed by the first or second shot which struck him?		
4 Was only Oswald involved in the assassination?		

Copy the table above. Look at the questions in Column 1. Fill each empty box with the views of the Warren Commission (Column 2) and the Select Committee (Column 3) on each question in Column 1. (One has already been done as an example.)

2   What are the most important differences between the two reports on Kennedy's assassination (Sources 3 and 4)? Explain your answer.

3   Can you suggest why the 1979 Select Committee report was prepared to state there probably *had* been a conspiracy to assassinate Kennedy while the Warren Commission claimed that there had *not* been a conspiracy?

4   What does the case of Kennedy's assassination show you about the problems of evidence in history?

6.4 The Kennedy myth

1 Why might the way in which someone dies affect the way in which they are judged by historians?

2 Can you think of other examples of public figures (e.g. politicians, actors, singers) who met an unexpected death, and around whom a myth has grown?

President Kennedy has probably had more books written about him than any other American President. The dramatic manner of his death, his youthful family, his attractive and cultured wife Jackie, and his relationships with many other women, all add up to an intensely interesting story on a human level. As a result, there has grown up about him a myth which can get in the way of assessing the *evidence* about his presidency.

Some historians claim that Kennedy was a great President. Others disagree. The problem is that evidence of Kennedy's actual achievements is not easy to find. Have historians been too easily misled by other issues, into helping to create the myth?

Below are different views of Kennedy from two historians. The first one is written by Howard Zinn, a left-wing historian. He specialises in writing about US history from the point of view of ordinary Americans – including, black people, women, American Indians and the poor. He writes of their struggle against powerful governments, injustice and intolerance.

Source 1

H. Zinn on Kennedy's record as President.

[On how the American people were not told the truth about the Bay of Pigs:]
Certain important news publications [newspapers] co-operated with the Kennedy administration in deceiving the American public on the Cuban invasion. The *New Republic* was about to print an article on the CIA training of Cuban exiles, a few weeks before the invasion. Historian Arthur Schlesinger was given copies of the article in advance. He showed them to Kennedy, who asked that the article be not printed, and the *New Republic* went along ....

[On the US treaty with the Indian Seneca people which guaranteed them the right to their land:]
But in the early sixties, under President Kennedy, the United States ignored the treaty and built a dam on this land, flooding most of the Seneca reservation.

William Manchester was an adviser to Kennedy during his presidency. In 1983 he published *Remembering Kennedy*. This extract is taken from that book:

Source 2

From W. Manchester, *Remembering Kennedy*, 1983.

This book is not a history. It is, quite simply, a book about him. In my opinion he was an exceptional man .... Perhaps his most appealing legacy lies in his compassion. He belonged to one of the wealthiest families in the United States, and he had not seen the misery of rock-bottom American poverty until the ... spring of 1960. Deeply moved, he made his first official act as President ... doubling the food rations of four million needy Americans. Later he launched Medicare and strengthened social security.
... On June 19, 1963, JFK sent a comprehensive [thorough] and far-reaching civil rights bill to Congress, thereby becoming the first president since Lincoln to put the full force of his office behind racial equality ....

The President's death was tragic, but his life had been a triumph, and that is how he should be remembered, and celebrated, now.

Questions

1 What two criticisms of Kennedy does Howard Zinn make in Source 1?

2 Which of Zinn's criticisms do you think is the most serious? Why?

3 Quote evidence from Source 2 to show how William Manchester is more favourable towards Kennedy.

4 Would you agree with Manchester's comment that Kennedy 'put the full force of his office behind racial equality' (Source 2)? Use evidence from the text to support your view.

5 How do you explain the fact that the historians Zinn and Manchester (Sources 1 and 2) have such different views about Kennedy?

6. 5 Review activity

Kennedy: your assessment of the President

Your assignment here is to assess Kennedy's performance as President.

Statement on Kennedy	Evidence for:	Evidence against:	My view (with explanation):
1 Kennedy achieved a great deal for the civil rights of black people.			
2 Kennedy successfully defended American interests abroad.			
3 The economy prospered under Kennedy.			
4 Kennedy's reputation as a great president is justified.			

1 Copy the chart above.

2 In Column 1 there are four positive statements about Kennedy. Your task is to find evidence which *supports* these statements (Column 2), and evidence which *disagrees* (Column 3). In Column 4 you have a chance to give *your* opinion of the statement and your reasons. Remember to use evidence to support your opinions.

Unit 7 · The United States since 1963

The 'American Dream' lives on

Source 1

The United States is as divided as ever between rich and poor. The extremes of wealth and poverty can be seen in this photograph of Washington in the 1990s.

The United States entered the First World War as the world's greatest economic power. By 1963 it was also the world's greatest military power, though the Soviet Union was not far behind. Since the collapse of the Soviet Union in 1991 it has become the world's only superpower, and the threat of nuclear war between the superpowers has faded.

Americans in 1963 were the richest they had ever been – they had 44 per cent more to spend in real terms than they had in 1929. However, this prosperity was unevenly spread. There was widespread poverty – among whites as well as blacks. In 1959 the government's own statistics stated that 22 per cent of all Americans lived below the poverty line; by 1968 this figure had dropped to 13 per cent. It was expected that the dynamic American economy would make poverty extinct in a short time but by 1992 the percentage of those below the poverty line had risen to 14 per cent, and the percentage of black poor had not changed from the 1968 level of 33 per cent.

Whilst many Americans enjoyed and continue to enjoy the highest standards of living in the world, there were critics of the 'American way'. Some, like the evangelist Billy Graham, believed that the lack of real Christian faith and the American obsession with consuming more of everything was at the heart of the problem:

Source 2

Billy Graham speaking in the 1950s, quoted in J. P. Diggins, *The Proud Decades*, 1989.

We overeat, overdrink, oversex, and overplay .... We have tried to fill ourselves with science and education, with better living and pleasure ... but we are still empty and bored.

The youth of the 1960s made a dramatic effort to find something better in America. Their protests against the war in Vietnam, their peace culture, flowers and 'love-ins' were part of this search, but they left the United States more divided than before. New racial divisions could be added to those of the black Americans. In the last few decades, Hispanic Americans from Puerto Rico, Mexico and Cuba have also been waking up to the fact that the American Dream has somehow passed them by.

Sources 1 and 3 suggest that the divisions in American society which have been traced in this book still exist today.

Source 3

Race riot in Los Angeles, 1992. Racial divisions and inequalities are still a noticeable feature of American life. Tensions can flare into open violence, as in this recent riot in California.